The Songs

By Janet L. Sharp

TEACH Services, Inc.
P U B L I S H I N G
www.TEACHServices.com

Copyright © 2012 TEACH Services, Inc.
ISBN-13: 978-1-57258-734-8 (Paperback)
ISBN-13: 978-1-57258-733-5 (Hardback)
ISBN-13: 978-1-57258-734-2 (ePub)
ISBN-13: 978-1-57258-823-3 (Kindle)
Library of Congress Control Number: 2011941912

Published by
TEACH Services, Inc.
P U B L I S H I N G
www.TEACHServices.com

Acknowledgments

This book would not have been possible to write without the meticulous records and photographs kept and preserved for our family by my grandmother, nor could it have been possible to write without the help of many family members who provided additional documentation and help in collecting further family records and information—and who also generously shared their memories. This collective information provided the basis for writing the story of my grandfather's life, which has been, as much as possible, reconstructed according to the known facts and memories shared with me.

Special acknowledgment must also be given to the church clerk of the Hackensack, Minnesota, Seventh-day Adventist Church for her generous help in providing information on the history of the Hackensack Seventh-day Adventist Church.

I gratefully thank everyone who contributed to the success of being able to write this story. This story is my gift to each member of my family, to those who knew my grandfather, and to those who would have loved knowing him.

Dedication

This book is dedicated with love to my parents, John and Muriel Sharp, for all they shared with me in life about faith, hope, and love. I will forever be grateful for the wonderful blessing of having them as my parents.

Contents

Prologue

It was a bright spring day now almost fifty years ago. The long, luscious row of lilacs was in full bloom some thirty yards west of the white barn door. Nostalgia lingered on the Minnesota farm, for the optimistic man with light blue eyes and crinkly lines around them that moved into smiles was gone.

His death came as a shock to my family—unexpected—full of grief. I was his first grandchild, just about to turn seven years old. On that spring day, standing with other family members in the fork of the dirt driveway that led to either the house or the barn, I gathered together and tucked into my heart my memories of Grandpa. He was a jovial man with a fascinating accent that accompanied his speech when he talked. The homemade cinnamon toast he often served for breakfast was my favorite—it tasted so scrumptious. Grandpa definitely knew how to bake.

Other memories about him tumbled around in my head—like the tender times he had held me on his lap, singing melodies in words from another place and language I was not familiar with, but curious about. I remembered being in church with him and hearing him energetically sing the hymns with a joyful devotion. Yes, my grandpa loved songs, and singing them. But now, I would never see him walk from the house to the barn and back again, taste the wonderful food he prepared, get to ask him questions I had wanted to ask him, sit on his lap, or get to hear his voice sing another song. The gently perfumed air from the lilacs and the sunny sky that day were such a contrast to the sad faces of family members and the emptiness we felt.

And yet today, saying "Grandpa" brings back a kaleidoscope of memories that still cause me to pause and marvel at the man who was my grandfather. The strength and faithfulness imbedded into his character and his friendship with Jesus were traits passed on to the lives of his children and to those whom he touched in his community and church. As the years passed, I learned interesting stories about his life, and I would always wonder what it would have been like to ask him about his personal experiences. And as I would listen to and ask about the stories told surrounding his life, time would somehow stand still as I pondered them.

For me, Grandpa's life continues to live on through the stories of a life full of storms and trials, of sunshine and providence, of faith, hope, and love. His life continues whenever I hear the songs he loved to sing—songs with words that reflect a God who has a plan for human lives. Grandpa's life continues when I take the time to ponder how God always led him along life's path—for there, God's hand of providence is uniquely observable.

Here are Grandpa's stories—all tangled up with water, storms, craggy rocks, homelands, and cares. Writing this book has taken me on a journey, a patchwork journey through time as I talked to family members and read and sorted through documents pertaining to his life. I then weaved the patchwork quilt of stories together into *The Songs*, the life story of my beloved grandfather as if he were recounting the details of his life while I was sitting on his lap nearly fifty years ago. These stories have become my lifetime friends and have filled me with hope—the kind that Grandpa had. Now, it is my turn to share the stories with you.

"But in your great mercy you did not put an end to them or abandon them, for you are a gracious and merciful God."
Nehemiah 9:31

Faith

Grandpa's Story

I didn't always live in America. My first homeland is a magical place packed with dense forests and thousands of lakes, rivers, and ponds—its coastline mostly surrounded by the sea. Water and trees—in profound abundance—are subject to winters so cold that the water lies frozen and the trees and ground are laden with snow for many months each year. About one fourth of the country is positioned within the Arctic Circle. In this country, nature balances harsh weather with a beauty one can only begin to describe. Finland is an enchanted land. This is where I was born.

I lived with my sister, four years older than I, and my parents in unbelievably poor circumstances. My father spent much of his time drinking alcohol. The meager income he earned mostly purchased his alcohol and continually left our family in desperate circumstances.

We lived in an abandoned Finnish bathhouse called a *savusana*. It was tightly constructed of logs forming one small room inside lined with benches of different heights. The floor was really a platform built up about three steps off the ground. There were no windows—only a single opening in the roof. Here the smoke could escape from the fire in the oven, which heated fist-sized red rocks uniquely built above the fire. When the rocks were very hot, the roof opening would be closed to retain steam in the room, which was created when water was poured over the hot rocks. This was how the bathhouse worked before it had been abandoned and became the structure where my family lived. Somehow, my mother re-made the old bathhouse into a home for our family.

It was nearing Christmas in the year of 1893. I had just turned two years old. Daylight hours in December were very short, and the temperature outside was way below zero. Day after day icy winter winds surged off the cold Baltic Sea and swirled around our tiny log structure we called home. Dense snowflakes fell intermittently in silent whispers outside. Luckily, wood was plentiful, and the old fire oven, with its now blackened rocks above it, still worked to bring heat into our home, while the smoke escaped from the small opening in the roof.

On one of those very cold winter days before Christmas, my mother learned from the county officials that my father was dead. He hadn't made it home the night before; his frozen body had been found in a snowdrift only a half mile from our old log home. Alcohol was the perpetrator, and his liver had failed from its provocation. Alcohol's fierce stranglehold had finally taken my father's life. Now, my mother was left alone with two young children to care for—and she was three months pregnant with twins. There was no income anymore, no matter how meager it had been, and no widow's pension left by my father. She was destitute and life's responsibilities were suddenly overwhelming.

I remember my mother's soft round face. Her long hair was always pulled back into a bun at the back of her head. The softness of her face almost concealed the despair and grief that her blue eyes betrayed. In spite of the circumstances, she held her head high—her jaw line was set with a fortitude borne of resilient determination. Socially, the times were difficult for the citizens of Finland—times which began to foster a period of staunch resistance against the Russian government of which Finland was subject.

To complicate the hardships even more, my mother was living in a nightmare that seemed to reveal a very frightening future for her young children. It was the dead of winter. What was my mother to do in order to survive? She had two children under the age of seven and was also pregnant with twins. Each day Mother would bundle me up along with my sister and push us on a sled from house to house begging for food. All winter and into the spring she begged for food to keep us alive, every week her girth expanding with the pregnancy. In time, no one offered their help. Her options at keeping us alive were depleted.

The Finnish government had a foster care program during those years. Under certain circumstances the county officials would set up an auction to sell children to the highest bidder. In this way, children of pitifully poor parents could be given the opportunity to have a better life and be taken care of. Some of the auction money went to help the poor parents survive and the rest went to the county. With a broken heart, my mother went to the county officials and arranged for an auction to take place. There was no other way out from these circumstances.

When the day for the auction arrived, my mother was there with me in her arms. She held me tightly, listening and watching intently to the bidders who had assembled. As the auctioneer continued driving up the price for me, a young couple finally stepped up and made the highest bid. They came forward and paid the officials the money. Then my mother handed me to their outstretched arms. I was now two and a half years old. I knew who my mother was and didn't want to leave her arms for those of the strangers.

My mother was insistent that arrangements be made for her to be able to keep in touch with me. Her strong will asserted itself in the midst of this anguish. She had done her best to give me a chance at life, but at great heartache to herself. The young couple graciously agreed to an arrangement of communicating by letter. My mother's soft face vanished from my sight on that day as she left the auction to return home. Her eyes were brimming with tears. She felt defeated and irresponsible for being unable to care for her own child.

All too soon, she would have two babies to auction come summertime. She dreaded feeling the grief and shame again when the necessity of those days would arrive. They, too, would have to be sold. Each baby had to have a chance to stay alive. Then she would find menial work to do in order to ensure her own survival and have some money to be able to keep in touch with her children by letter. My sister was old enough to stay with her while she worked, and so she decided that she could keep at least one precious child while earning a living.

My new home was a farmhouse on another island in the Baltic Sea, which required a ferryboat ride from the town where I had lived with my mother. It was a modest two-story farmhouse, fixed simply, but cozy inside. The outside of the house was covered with large, rough shingles that lined its four sides. There was an adjacent barn for the cows and work horses not far from the back of the house. Behind the barn you could see dense rows of coniferous forests. These led to the waters that contain one of the world's most beautiful archipelagoes. Thousands of islands dot these waters—waters filled with rocky crags forming a tangled maze that requires great skill to navigate by boat.

The fens and bogs of these Finnish coastlines are home to numerous species of water birds and waders. And near the water's shores were bounteous areas for hunting wild mushrooms and picking wild lingonberries during late summer and autumn. Along the shorelines were forests of the dark pyramid-shaped forms of the Norway Spruce that held the nests of eagles and owls. These trees, with their spreading branches and long, pendulous cones, were a magnificent sight in winter when heavily loaded with snow.

I remember watching the spectacular sunrises and sunsets along the shorelines of the islands, each one different as the days and seasons changed. I felt peace and contentment with the nature that surrounded me, and as the years went by, safe with the love and care of my kind foster parents.

The Songs

My foster parents were devout Christians in the Lutheran Church, which had been established in Finland since the sixteenth century. Each week I went to Sunday School and church. Prayer before eating a meal and also at bedtime were customary in our home. My foster parents were both very kind and loving toward me. Little by little, I learned from them that there was a God who loved and cared about people on this earth. To this day, my gratitude continues for the direction and care of my foster parents. I love them for the care they gave to me and was blessed by the fortunate circumstances of being able to learn about God from them.

Christmas traditions are well established and important in Finland. These traditions go back to the Middle Ages and are celebrated throughout Finland. On Christmas Eve in the town squares, Martin Luther's hymn "A Mighty Fortress Is Our God" is sung and then Luther's "Declaration of Christmas Peace" is read out loud.

I vividly remember a story that my foster mother told me on Christmas Eve before I went to bed when I was four years old. Somehow, deep down, I could relate to the story even though I was very young. It is a story I have never forgotten. Let me share this story with you, just as I remember hearing her tell it to me.

> "Once upon a time, long, long ago, there was a father and a son. This father loved his precious son very much. There was a really important job that the father needed his son to do. But, in order to accomplish this important job, he would need to send his son far, far away from

home. It would be many years before he would be able to see his son again. This made the father exceptionally sad, for he would need to place his son in someone else's care. His son would have to go and live in a new home, very different from his home with his father.

"The day came when the little baby boy was given to his new mother. There were barn animals nearby when he arrived and was placed in his new mother's arms. There were strangers near to welcome him. He had a new father too.

"His new mother loved him very much, and from the time he was very small, she never let a day go by that she would tell him about his real father. She told him that his father was far, far away, but that he loved him so much and would find ways to keep in touch with him as he grew up. Someday, his father would be able to see him again. All the boy had to do was believe that his father would never forget him and would keep his promises.

"The little boy continued to grow, and every day he thought about his father. They did find ways to keep in touch with each other, and their trust and friendship grew stronger as the years went by.

"This little boy's name was Jesus. He left a comfortable home in heaven to come to this earth to accomplish a mission. His Father's name was God. The boy's new home was a place on earth—in an area named after a very large lake called Galilee. Jesus spent a lot of time in a boat on this lake and also along the shores of the lake. His mission involved people—lots of people.

"Jesus and God did miss each other very much while Jesus was in Galilee, but They both knew that the mission was very important. They had great faith in each other that their mission would be accomplished and then Jesus would be able to return home to His Father. And, this *is* what happened a long, long time ago.

"Today, Jesus is back in heaven with God, after He spent thirty-three years of being away from His Father. Someday, I will tell you stories about Their mission and about Jesus' life near Galilee. But for now, what you need to remember about this story is that the mission involved Jesus' love for people—and that includes you."

While growing up, my foster mother told me stories from the Bible about Jesus' mission. She told me the stories about His life near Galilee while He was here on this earth. I learned more about these stories at church, but I especially enjoyed learning them from my foster mother. When I was twelve years old, I was confirmed into the Lutheran Church. That was a special day for me at church, for I was certain that I had a real Friend in heaven, a Friend who understood my life, a Friend who had a foster mother like I did.

My birth mother did keep in touch with me. Whenever her letters arrived in the mail, my foster mother would read them to me until I was able to read on my own. I was very fortunate to have two mothers who loved me. After I was a grown man, I was able to find my birth mother and spend some time with her. She told me about the difficult days of having to send me away to another home. But I understood. Another boy, a long, long time ago had also lived that experience. I had learned how to have faith because that boy had shown me how.

What I didn't yet understand was what my mission in life was to be. I really hadn't been thinking about it too hard until change was imposed upon my comfortable life. In just a few weeks, I was to complete grammar school. One evening my foster parents came to me and kindly told me that when I graduated from grammar school I would be old enough to earn my own living. Their foster care responsibilities would be legally ended. I would have to leave the farmhouse and learn how to live the rest of my life without their financial support. They promised to help me find work. But the perplexity of the situation hit me hard, and I struggled to make sense of the impending changes. What was I to do with these new conditions soon to affect my life?

After graduating from the eighth grade in the spring of 1904, I was hired by some neighbors to help them with their farm work and fishing. The schedule for these two jobs was grueling. I would begin my day at four o'clock in the morning with the fishing crew. We would fish until breakfast. When breakfast was finished, I would join the farm crew and work in the fields caring for the crops all day. The growing season lasted for about four months in Finland, so we worked diligently to take advantage of the season's short timeline. The fields were small because the land was disrupted by the forests and water inlets, so we had many land areas to plow, plant, till, and harvest.

After working in the fields, I would again join the fishing crew and go night fishing. We would set up our boat where we planned to fish for the night, eat some supper, and then wait for the fish. Some nights we caught a lot of fish in our nets, and on others, very few. I learned how to deftly maneuver the fishing boat around the big boulders in the brackish water to where the fish were located while also keeping an eye on the horizon, hoping to get a few nods of blessed sleep before early morning arrived. I learned how to pull in the nets loaded with fish and how to store the fish for market the next day. After a night of very little sleep, we would begin our day again at four o'clock in the morning—often at another location—with another fishing round before breakfast.

When winter came, ice fishing out on the frozen waters was our work. It was unmercifully cold with temperatures hovering near zero degrees and even colder when the wind would blow. Snow would fall often, and we would have to make new tracks back to the frozen water each day.

This schedule was extremely difficult for me. I was only twelve years old and wasn't as strong as the men I worked for. As the days of each season relentlessly came and went, one after the other, I realized I could not keep up with this kind of a schedule. I was always exhausted from hard work, difficult weather, and lack of meaningful sleep. After five years of these harsh and taxing work conditions as a teenager, I began to think about what other work I could do. I was now seventeen years old, and the demanding farming and night fishing days of summer were underway once again.

My foster father had taught me some skills in carpentry, so I decided to apply for training at a vocational school to learn cabinetmaking. This gave me a goal to reach and for the rest of the summer I anxiously waited for the classes to begin.

When school opened that autumn, there was no room for me in the cabinetmaking class. The class had been filled, and my application was rejected for that school year. I was desperate and extremely disappointed. What was I to do next? Thinking about another long, cold, punishing winter of ice fishing brought my spirits into feelings of hopelessness. But, determined to succeed, I pressed on.

It took a week of searching in-between my other jobs to find another opportunity for vocational training. The only program that had room for me in the class was at a cooking school in Turku, Finland. The program taught students how to be a steward on board a ship. The country island that I was used to—the lakes and tree-lined shores with the coastline of safety around it—would no longer be my refuge. Oh, how I loved the solitude and beauty of the country. Would I ever be able to return to the safety of the island again?

Now, due to tough choices and limited opportunities, I would be going to a big city to learn to do something I had never done before—cook. I wasn't used to city life; however, I knew I couldn't manage the exhausting schedules of both fishing and farming in order to survive. Everything in my life had turned upside down.

And so, with a heavy heart, feeling like I was on the brink of disaster, my thoughts turned to my Friend in heaven. I remember earnestly wondering how He had figured out His mission when He lived in Galilee, was on the lake in a boat, or walking the shores and countryside. How had his Father guided Him through it all so He could do His important job? I couldn't seem to find an answer for my own circumstances that helped me understand anything about my destiny.

I had never longed so much for the warm arms and comforting hugs and encouragement of my foster mother as I did during those uncharted moments of my life. She wasn't there to help me now, but through her diligent influence in my upbringing, she had helped me to catch a glimpse of how to trust. Because I had a high regard for my Friend in heaven, I was able to maintain the determination to hang on—even though silence seemed to be keeping an answer from me. Although I felt encumbered with mountains of disappointment and felt as if I was on the very border of despair, I was still sure that an answer would come. At least I had a class to attend. That was more than I had the previous week as an option.

I left life on the island and began classes at the cooking and stewardship school in Turku in September 1909. Turku is Finland's oldest city and was founded in the thirteenth century. It is also the busiest seaport in Finland and was the first capital city of Finland until Helsinki officially became the capital in 1812 after Finland was ceded by Sweden to Imperial Russia in 1809.

And so, this is where and how the first seventeen years of my life were lived. I loved Finland. The beauty of nature was astonishing. Water was fundamentally responsible for this abundant beauty, and for my livelihood. Finland is where I was introduced to faith through a friendship with Jesus—

despite unfortunate beginnings.

When I became a young man in my thirties, I learned the song "Memories of Galilee." Whenever I sing the words, I think of the delightful Finnish island that was my home, and I also wonder how Jesus feels now whenever He remembers His home in Galilee.

"Each cooing dove and sighing bough,

That makes the eve so blessed to me,

Has something far diviner now,

It bears me back to Galilee.

"Each flowery glen and mossy dell,

Where happy birds in songs agree,

Through sunny morn the praises tell,

Of sights and sounds in Galilee.

"And when I read the thrilling lore,

Of Him who walked upon the sea,

I long, oh, how I long once more,

To follow Him in Galilee.

The Songs

"O Galilee, sweet Galilee,

Where Jesus loved so much to be,

O Galilee, blue Galilee,

Come sing thy song again to me." [1]

~~~~~~~~~~~~~~~~~~~~~~~~~~~~~~~~~~~~~~~

Of course, there is more about faith that my Friend, Jesus, taught me to understand. While He was in Galilee accomplishing His mission, He longed for His real home. He made a promise about His real home. He promised that His real home is the very same home I can live in one day. Faith lets you believe in what seems, at times, to be impossible. Faith is a gift you may choose to hold and cherish in all circumstances of life.

There's no disappointment in heaven,

No weariness, sorrow or pain;

No hearts that are bleeding and broken,

No song with a minor refrain.

The clouds of our earthly horizon

---

1   Robert Morris, "Memories of Galilee," (1874).

Will never appear in the sky,

For all will be sunshine and gladness,

With never a sob nor a sigh.

I'm bound for that beautiful city,

My Lord has prepared for His own;

Where all the redeemed of all ages

Sing 'Glory!' around the white throne;

Sometimes I grow homesick for heaven,

And the glories I there shall behold;

What a joy that will be when my Savior I see,

In that beautiful city of gold![2]

My Story

Through the years of my life, I have carefully pondered Grandpa's story. I began to understand how magnetic water and homelands can be. They each exude their own energy

___

[2] Frederick M. Lehman, "There's No Disappointment in Heaven," (1914).

that draws the human soul toward a longing for permanence. However, permanence can be an illusion when directed earthward. Only faith can keep the energies alive when the longed for permanence is directed heavenward.

*" 'They will be mine,' says the LORD Almighty, 'in the
day when I make up my treasured possession. I will
spare them, just as in compassion a man spares his own
son who serves him.'" Malachi 3:17*

Hope

Grandpa's Story

Cooking school turned out to be an enjoyable experience.
I did very well in my classes over the next months as I
attended the school. I was able to make a living in Turku
by working at a bakery very early in the morning. Then, I
attended classes at the school. I have always enjoyed learning.
Even though cooking and baking were things I had never
dreamed of learning about, I did take a liking to these skills,
and I especially became fond of baking.

I graduated from cooking school with distinction and
received my diploma in April 1910. When September came,
it was necessary for me to apply for a passport, for my first
job was to be as mess attendant preparing meals on a Finnish
merchant ship that sailed between Scandinavia and Germany.

Ship life in those days was known to be a rough life—not only because of the perils of sea travel but because of the drunkenness and depravity of many men who sailed the seas. For myself, I had an aversion to drinking. I knew well the story of my father's obsession with it. My birth mother's letters had described the conditions of my father's death and how alcohol had forever ruined all chances of my family unit being able to stay together. Her anguish remained as she did her best to communicate why she had been forced to give me away. I was determined to never crave or need the companionship of this damaging habit. Fighting and swearing were actions that I was unfamiliar with as well. My foster parents had discouraged these behaviors and would not allow them to be present in our home, for they did not coincide with attributes of a Christian life.

My birth mother was distraught when I wrote to tell her of my new employment. In her reply letter, she begged and pleaded with me to reconsider, for she knew about some of the predicaments I would encounter with life on board a ship. She had observed the lives of many merchant sailors—hardened by this rough life. They had the trophies of broken noses, busted knuckles, and other scars from the numerous brawls they had been in. Most had heavily imbibed their alcohol. Her fear for my future was very real to her.

Despite her disappointment and fears, I forged ahead with my plans, relieved that I had discovered a way to make a living I enjoyed. I trusted my personal values to stay firm as choices would come along the way. In fact, I had acknowledged my gratefulness many times to my Friend in heaven for His help in unfolding the mission for my life. I just couldn't let

Him down now after these comfortable circumstances had revealed themselves. Privately, within my own heart, I knew that answers about my future had been given. And so, I was drawn by this compassionate disclosure and remained fixed on being loyal to it. My hope for the future was strong.

I was comfortable being on the water. However, I was used to being on small fishing boats in waters that were near the shoreline. I remember looking out through the galley porthole and watching the shoreline of Finland fade farther and farther away as our ship, the *Rhea*, left Finland that autumn morning of my first sea journey. Even though this vessel was large, I could feel the waves of the sea begin to swell about the ship, and I could hear the wind intensely beating on the large square-rigged sails held by the three masts that directed the *Rhea's* course. The sounds and movement were a bit disconcerting, but I had a noon meal to prepare. And so, I busied myself, becoming acquainted with the galley and how to work efficiently in it.

As that first day of sailing the open sea came to a close and night began to descend upon us, all I could see through the porthole was water, water, and more water. Every now and then a sea bird could be seen steering its course alongside the ship. I wondered how they could travel so far from land. A feeling of isolation came over me, and for that moment, I began to feel so insignificant in comparison to the vastness of the water holding up our ship. I strangely noticed that my homeland could only be seen in my mind's eye, for I was nowhere near its safe borders. In time, new shorelines appeared and then disappeared while the *Rhea* came and went through the ports of call of Norway, Sweden, Denmark, and

Germany that first year I sailed on her.

When August 1911 arrived, we were busy making plans to take a much longer voyage than the short ones we had been taking the previous year. New trade connections had been made for our ship to travel to. On a lovely autumn day in early September, the *Rhea* left the port of Rauma, Finland, sailed up the coast of Finland to Jakobstad to load more trading goods, and then turned back to sea to sail for London.

We were to be in the port of London for a month, so I took the opportunity to catch a train to Hull, England. Over the centuries of time, Hull had developed into a major British trade port with mainland Europe. In 1911 the city was a borough within the lovely Yorkshire region of England. It was named for the Hull River, which is a tributary to the River Humber, an inlet to the North Sea. I chose to make this trip to Hull because this was where I could attend the Board of Trade School for cooks and stewards and then take the Board of Trade Examination. The captain of our ship agreed with my intentions and promised an increase in pay for passing the exam since this would enable me to be an additional asset to the ship's crew.

Taking this exam was something I had wanted to personally accomplish, because it would give me a new ranking as steward on ships that sailed around the world. Not only would I be able to prepare the meals aboard ship but I would become the ship's officer who was in charge of provisions and dining arrangements. Before leaving land to sail to our destinations, my new responsibilities would include carefully planning the menus and keeping meticulous records of the amount of food needed to ensure an adequate supply of food to feed the crew until we could restock our supplies the next time we docked in port. Any special dining needs for the ship's captain on our voyages would also be my responsibility. I have always been motivated to better myself and improve my skills as opportunities present themselves. This was one of them.

I studied hard and passed the Board of Trade Examination and returned to London in time to make the necessary preparations needed for the *Rhea* to cross the Atlantic Ocean, destined for Haiti in the Caribbean Sea. I wasn't sure what it would be like to be on the water for weeks at a time without seeing land, but I was soon to find out.

The Atlantic Ocean is the world's second largest ocean, covering about one-fifth of the earth's surface. It is known for the dangerous and sometimes difficult crossings in the North Atlantic waters during the winter months. However, our captain chose to travel during the winter months to avoid the persistent fog and hurricane threats of the other months. We experienced frequent squalls of sudden winds accompanied by rain. The ship would pitch and creak, displacing items in the galley that weren't firmly in place. Many times I had to clean up the mess left in the galley from these disruptive encounters with nature. Then, just as abruptly as the squall had arrived, it would leave. The skies would again be clear, and the sun would once again smile upon the expanse of waters.

The galley was the perfect place for me to be on ship. I could prepare meals and clean up after meals while being left alone to keep the process going for my shipmates and captain. Three times a day I was responsible to serve tasty meals. My lightheartedness and sense of humor made it easy for me to adjust to the occasional jesting and ridicule

I sometimes received about the meals. There was usually a bully who enjoyed being obnoxious about anything they had a fancy to use as bait for a fight. I paid no heed and kept doing my job despite these occasional interruptions. Since I was now an officer and the only cook on board ship, I wasn't bothered very often. The cook was necessary if they wanted their meals. And sailors wanted their meals.

It was absolutely delightful to come upon the islands in the Caribbean Sea. The warm, tropical January air and turquoise water surrounding sandy beaches lined with swaying palm trees stunned the senses of this hardy sailor who was used to the unsympathetic cold of winters in Finland. But the *Rhea* wasn't to stay long in this paradise, and when our business in Haiti had been accomplished, the captain redirected the sails to again cross the Atlantic Ocean where we landed finally at the port of Dunkirk, France. From there we sailed up to Sweden for a brief stop before crossing the familiar Baltic Sea back to Finland.

By the time we deported the ship, spring was just showing its promises of warmer days. I took leave to go and visit my foster parents on the idyllic island that had been my home. Riding the ferryboat and feeling the air of the Baltic Sea breezing across my face was so welcome.

It was heartwarming to see my foster parents again, along with friends and comrades I had once worked beside. I shared with them the experiences of my employment and travels, and they listened and asked questions in abundance.

The sights, sounds, and smells of the familiar island environment brought rejuvenation to my soul. It was a treat to have someone else do the cooking, and being able to eat the favorite foods of my childhood again was delightful. I spent most of the summer on the island, helping with much of the farming and fishing, but this time the tasks did not exhaust me.

When it was time to say good-bye, my foster mother put her arms around me and held me tightly. While we stood together in this embrace, she told me that she was very proud of me. I remember her kind voice telling me that she would continue praying for me on my upcoming voyages upon the sea. She would also be praying that I would remain steadfast in my Christian beliefs to the Lutheran faith.

I thanked her and softly reminded her that the stories she had told me long ago about Galilee were still very much a part of my life. I reassured her that I intended to stay committed to God—my esteem for God and my faith were high. I told her I always carried the Bible she had given me when I was confirmed into the Lutheran Church and that it went across the waters with me. I will never forget the look of peace and contentment on her face after we had this touching exchange and left each other's embrace. My foster mother was one of the jewels in my life.

It was now September 1912. I received orders that I was being transferred to the Finnish ship *Njord* and would continue as steward aboard this merchant vessel. Once again, I began making preparations for the upcoming voyage, which would take us back to the Caribbean Sea—this time to Cuba.

When November arrived and the weather was becoming harshly cold, we left Finland's port of Kotka on the Njord. This three-mast vessel set its square-rigged sails for London and then across the rough waters of the Atlantic toward the splendid beauty of the Caribbean Sea. It took me a couple of days to adjust to the new galley, and then the daily duties flowed smoothly one after the other. Day after day and night after night we pressed on toward our destination during the months that best eliminated experiencing the most known hazardous weather patterns. We encountered the usual brief snarly winter storms that seemed to spontaneously arise out of nowhere. The clouds were either dark and luminous, gold-rimmed, or completely absent in the immense skies above the ocean.

By late winter we arrived again in Europe, this time at the major German ports of Bremen and then Hamburg, before sailing to our home port in Finland. Germany's northern ports of Bremen and Hamburg both have histories that are centuries long, dating back to medieval times. They were key commercial trade ports where Germany's merchant ships dominated the main trade routes of the North Sea and the Baltic Sea between Europe and Scandinavia. By 1900 Hamburg had experienced tremendous growth, mainly due to the trade routes that had developed across the Atlantic Ocean. Hamburg had become the third-largest port in Europe, and it was always bustling.

I decided to take some time during the summer of 1913 to find and visit my birth mother for the first time since she had given me away. I was a bit apprehensive but felt deep inside that this was something I had to do. If not someday, why not now, I figured. I wasn't afraid of her, just comfortable with the relationship we had developed through letter writing. I kept thinking, why change anything that was comfortable? However, I had the opportunity now, so I found the courage to make contact with her in person.

It was a surprise to her when I showed up at the door of her little cottage where she now lived. Summer flowers were blooming at the front of the cottage under the windows. Soft curtains could be seen silhouetted against the windows from the morning light outside. A gentle breeze blew in the warm air. I remember her eyes matching the bright blue of the sky that morning as I looked into them and said, "Hello, Mother. I am Kustaa, your son."

She was so warm toward me, and without hesitation she threw her arms around me. I felt the sobs that began to gently shake her body as she held on to me tightly. There was a huge lump in my throat, and I felt the tears stinging my eyes. When I regained my composure and could talk, I continued holding her and said, "It's OK, Mother. I understand about the past. Really, I do. Please don't hold on to any remorse about it. Thank you for keeping in touch with me by letter for all these years. You'll never know how much your letters have meant to me. You have always been my mother. Now that I am grown up, I'd like to come and visit you often and make new memories with you."

And so, I spent a week with my mother, catching up on our lives and renewing our bond together. I remember her curiosity about an incident that had happened to me when I was around nine years old. Somehow she knew a few details about an accident I had had on the ice and wanted to know more about it. So I told her the story.

During the winter months, we had to cross the frozen water by skates or skis in order to get to our school. Back and forth on the ice I would go each day to and from school with my friends. As the days nearing springtime arrived before school was out, the water was still quite solidly frozen; however, one day as I was skating across the ice, it cracked, and I immediately fell into the icy water. My friends were ahead of me and didn't notice my plight. I tried my best to climb out of the water, only to fall back into the icy water. Three times I did my best to get out of the water and back onto the ice above. I was very cold and was losing my strength.

Finally, one of my friends noticed I was missing and came back to find me. He called out to the others to bring a large stick, and together my friends pulled me out of the water while I tightly gripped the stick. I remember them sharing their coats, mittens, and woolen caps with me. Then they got me back home where my foster mother put me in the steaming sauna, gave me some hot soup, and tucked me into a warm bed. I ended up with a few aches and pains, and my foster mother never let me forget that God had taken care of me and spared my life, for she believed that there was something special He had planned for me.

After finishing the story, I noticed by the expression on her face that my mother's instinct had been right—she had always suspected that something life-threatening had happened to me. For all these years she had wondered what had really happened to her little boy. I guess my foster mother had been careful about how many of the details of this incident she had given in her letters to my birth mother so as not to alarm her. In their own ways, they each had acted out of love and concern for me—for they were my mothers.

My mother shared stories with me, too. She told me that my older sister, Elli, was married and planning to emigrate to America with her husband. I learned that I had a younger brother, Pauli, who had already emigrated to Canada. My mother hadn't been able to see him before he had boarded the passenger ship and left; in fact, she hadn't seen Pauli since the day she also had to give him away. But the letters—he had kept in touch through letters—just like I had done all these years because our mother really cared about each one of her children.

I learned that Pauli had a twin sister, Anna, who still lived in Finland but was making plans to emigrate to Canada soon to be near Pauli. Anna and Pauli had been auctioned together to a foster family who had also agreed to keep in touch with our mother. While my mother had been unable to visit Anna in person, she still wrote letters to her as well. She gave me Anna's address. I was anxious to be in touch with her as soon as possible. I also wanted to visit Elli and her husband as soon as I could.

Our mother had been able to keep up with events that occurred in her children's lives without being able to be there with them. Her children were still her children, even though she hadn't raised us. Because of her tenacity to keep in touch, I was able to put the pieces of my life together. It was like assembling a quilt from old bits of fabric from days of old. I wondered how the fragments could be so well preserved and memories kindled so warmly. Only a mother could make that kind of magic happen.

My birth mother was very relieved that I had strong values that kept me from becoming hardened and raucous. I shared with her my beliefs in God and about how I felt He had been leading me. She listened carefully, pondering the things about

God's love for people on this earth from what I shared with her.

Although she listened to me explain my faith and how I felt God had led me, she unrelentingly clung to her concerns for my safety upon the sea—for nature could be cruel and nondiscriminating. However, I knew her concerns were there because she cared about me and loved me. All I could tell her was, "Mother, I truly trust in God. He will take care me." This special week with my birth mother was very fulfilling, and I will always be grateful that I took the time to find her and finally become acquainted with her in person. She was a very dear lady.

I returned to the *Njord* where preparations were underway to sail south to Barcelona, Spain. Our itinerary included stopping first at the port of Hamburg, Germany, and then Lisbon, Portugal, and Santa Cruz in the Canary Islands before passing through the Straits of Gibraltar to Barcelona. The *Njord* finally embarked on this journey in September. My thoughts were contemplative on this trip. I had received the addresses of my brother and two sisters from my mother. In my spare time, I began writing letters to them, telling them of my visit with our mother and also about my life as a steward aboard sailing vessels. I collected postcards of the ports we visited so I could share my adventures with them by mail, and I encouraged them to write to me and tell me about their lives.

On this voyage I spent more time on deck during the evening hours. I was stunned by the autumn sunsets that spread mile after endless mile along earth's bare horizon, leaving their russet, orange, and red reflections to bounce and shift upon the continual movement of the ocean waves. The whole ocean seemed to be transformed into acres and acres of burning hot coals each evening. And as the sun finally dropped silently out of sight, the dark grays and blues would return, capped with their tufts of white, which continued to break against the ships bow. The ship and the waves never slept. Both were integrally connected by the constant motion.

This connection gave me opportunity to think about the unpredictability that can be imposed upon the permanencies that one takes for granted. When the transformations are beautiful, it is a delight to experience. But what happens when the transformations became terrifying? How could one's hope find steadiness to confidently maintain a desired outcome under such circumstances? I wondered, but I didn't want to try and find any answers.

And so, the days and nights of our South Atlantic voyage to Spain passed one after the other until the *Njord* returned to Finland in the dead of winter, the week before Christmas. I remember hearing the surface ice of the Baltic Sea being broken up by our ship as it progressively moved closer to the harbor. Behind us remained millions of ice chunks floating in the *Njord's* wake. Turku was cold and covered with snow. I was home in beautiful Finland again.

When I picked up my mail at the ship's port, I had a postcard from Anna with her picture on it. She was such a pretty girl, and I was drawn by the fact that she was my real sister. I also had a letter waiting from my birth mother telling me that Anna had become very sick with pneumonia and had died that autumn. Now, the sister I had just received a glimpse of on the postcard was gone. I would never be able to see her pretty face in person. My heart was heavy, and I immediately set out to correspond with my mother about this tragic loss.

Christmas Eve was only a couple of days away. I made plans to attend the usual church services that would be held at the Lutheran Church I had attended in Turku while at cooking school. The snow was falling heavily that Christmas Eve. The sidewalks were slippery, and the biting wind was blowing. I was so preoccupied with walking carefully to the church and thinking of Anna with my head down and my face mostly covered with a woolen scarf to deflect the bitter cold that I bumped into another person at the corner where the sidewalks intersected.

Both of us promptly fell onto the slippery sidewalk. Looking over at the other person sprawled in the snow adjacent to me, I saw two beautiful green eyes staring with surprise into mine. Immediately, we both began apologizing profusely to each other and then broke out laughing at how humorous the situation really was. I stood up and quickly went over to help the young lady up onto her feet, asking if she was injured in any way. She smiled and asked the same of me, her eyes twinkling.

After we had brushed the snow off our coats and were satisfied we were each fine, I introduced myself. Then, I asked if I could escort her safely to the church—for that was also her destination. I held out my arm for her to loop hers through, and together we made our way to the Christmas Eve church services. When they were over, I boldly asked if I could escort her safely home. With a quick wit, she replied that maybe I was the one who needed to be safely escorted. Again, we laughed, remembering our earlier tumble in the snow. I did escort her home, and over the next few months we spent time together.

As I got ready to leave on another voyage, we exchanged pictures of each other and I promised to write when I could.

When spring arrived in 1914, I received notice from the ship's captain that I had been chosen for a promotion because of my loyalty, personal integrity, and capabilities proven as a steward on his ship the past three years. He was being transferred to Finland's largest merchant ship, the *Fennia*, and he wanted me to continue as steward aboard this vessel. As a reward, I was to be given the highest pay of all Finnish ship crew members at that time. This was a humbling experience. The privilege of having my heartfelt desire of not only finding but so far succeeding in my life's mission was a veritable reality. The nebulous and undefined perimeters of hope did have their way of manifesting into recognizable elements.

As I thought about the hope my Friend must have had while He was in Galilee—that He would be able to recognize and complete His mission without a written plan to follow—I began to understand the process of hope. Its results are revealed quietly and almost imperceptibly. They become discernible only when hope has been rewarded. In the meantime, I learned to confidently maintain hope in a desired outcome and then watch for its rewards to become visible.

And so, I became the steward on Finland's largest merchant ship. The *Fennia* had four masts hung with square-rigged sails that were set up for travel to the continents and countries south of the equator. Life on the ocean aboard a ship had become quite agreeable to me. I was enjoying the splendid opportunities of visiting so many areas of the world. And now, to have the chance to venture to places even farther away, brought me much joy and anticipation. I was almost twenty-three years old. I had a sweetheart. I was optimistic, happy, grateful for my employment, fond of the work I was doing, and was enjoying the stability of my life aboard ship. Little did I know that the upcoming voyage would be one that I would never forget—from start to finish.

In July 1914 we hastily began preparations for a long voyage to Australia and South America. I meticulously stocked the galley with a two-year supply of food staples for this trip in case our return was delayed by circumstances beyond our control. It was challenging to plan for and store as much of the perishable and nonperishable types of foods as possible that we would be needing for a trip this long. Climate changes would affect the storage of food greatly. Other factors affecting this trip were the chain of events that began rapidly happening across Europe while we were preparing for our voyage.

Indelibly etched into my memory are the conditions and dates upon which we began sailing on this voyage and the events that would unfold as our journey was being taken. When I reflect back now, the dates and events were so closely entwined with our ship's movements that only by looking back upon what was occurring can one appreciate the precariousness that followed our days upon the great oceans.

There had been a strong, nationalistic zeal intensifying within three imperial dynasties of Europe—the Hohenzollern family of Germany, the Habsburg family of Austria-Hungary, and the Romanov family of Russia. Each dynasty held grudges that had smoldered since the Congress of Vienna coalition back in 1815, which defeated France in the wars caused by Napoleon's attempt to dominate Europe. Also, each dynasty had held on to covert ambitions to be the greatest in military might, and each competed for colonization territories and industrial development. Each remained secretly hopeful of becoming the superior power in Europe, and each maintained detailed plans developed for this purpose.

For the previous twenty years, the nations of Europe had been developing a system of alliances in hopes of promoting and maintaining the peace that was subtly being threatened by the three aristocratic dynasties. However, this system of alliances backfired when a Serbian revolutionary fearlessly assassinated the heir to the Austria-Hungary throne, along with his wife, on June 28, 1914. Tensions immediately became extremely high all over Europe, and this assassination event began to trigger one country after another to declare war on the other, with loyal allies backing each other in the process.

Fearing that we would not be able to leave port if we waited any longer, our captain abruptly gave orders to immediately board the ship. It was midnight when our crew was aroused and told to get on board. We were to embark in two hours. In the dark of night, I watched the scattered lights of Finland's shoreline fade hastily away as the four massive sails stole the *Fennia* quietly out of the harbor, maneuvering its way across the Baltic Sea to Sweden's port of Sundsvall for a brief stop.

The *Fennia* promptly entered the sea waters and headed for the dark waters of the North Atlantic Ocean where the ship picked a course that led southward—within calculated margins to keep us safe from Europe's coastline. Part of our captain's security that night was founded in the knowledge that England had a superb navy of ships that would be guarding the North Sea and the English Channel, making passage to the Atlantic safe from any German sea attacks, for Germany had already invaded Belgium, causing England to declare war on Germany. Treacherous waters were to be the haunting threat that followed our beautiful ship on this voyage. We were unaware that Australia and New Zealand were already invading and taking control of German colonies for England in the South Pacific Ocean. And these were the distant waters where the *Fennia* was bound.

When I look back on the turbulent historical events that were in the process of taking place, I am amazed that our ship was safely in the Atlantic Ocean just one day before one of the bloodiest encounters between France and Germany, which began on August 14 with the invasion of Lorraine. We were not aware of it that morning when we rapidly left Finland way before dawn arrived. In only six days, the French had lost 140,000 men during this first Battle of the Frontiers. Other battles were raging and lives were being snuffed out.

On August 28 England sank and damaged several German naval ships in the first major naval battle fought in the North Sea near the island of Heligoland Bight. Germany lost 1,200 men in that sea battle. The Great War was furiously underway. Country after country had declared war, and the Allied Powers and Central Powers began the necessary military moves that would result in the loss of more than fifteen million lives by the time the war finally ended.

During the fifty years before the Great War began, more than three hundred thousand Finnish people had emigrated to America and Canada. When the war began, I was relieved that my brother, Pauli, was among them and was safely away from the European continent. Even though Russia was part of the Allied Powers at the beginning of the war, I had grave concerns about my family members in Finland. Would some of my friends have to join the Russian forces and fight against Germany? Would Finland remain safe from bombs and German occupation? Would I ever be able to traverse the waters that would take me home to Finland—waters that were now heavily guarded and sabotaged by military might?

What would happen to my sweetheart and to her family? Together we had discussed the shocking events unfolding across Europe. We had exchanged pictures and promised to wait for each other until I returned from my upcoming voyage. I wasn't able to say good-bye to her due to the hasty departure of my ship. I didn't know if I could mail letters to her from ports we would be stopping at. All I had was a picture of her and sentimental memories that endeared her to me.

My heart was heavy with the unknowns of the future. In the meantime, I was sailing for Australia. War had left life tempestuous and stormy. Each nation continued charting their own course as telegraph buttons frantically tapped the messages that flew back and forth along the communication lines. What now of hope? My stable life had suddenly become fragile and felt strangely out of control. What should I hope for now? Would I even live to have a future beyond today—or tomorrow? As wide and unending as the rough ocean waters the *Fennia* traversed, so were my growing doubts and fears.

Thankfully, the days passed without encountering difficulty. In the course of time, the *Fennia* left the summer season north of the equator and moved steadily toward the summer season of the southern hemisphere. This year would be one long summer as we would be experiencing both sides of the equator.

Somehow, being in the large open waters seemed to bring a sense of safety from the traumas of war occurring on land. In October we received word from a friendly passing merchant vessel that Australia and New Zealand ships had been successful in securing the ocean waters in those regions from German control by mid-September. Australia was determined to fight for England and had begun an aggressive offensive in early August. This left our voyage in relatively safe conditions as we made our way southward from Europe.

We sailed approximately nine thousand five hundred miles before rounding the southern tip of Africa where the *Fennia* entered the waters of the warm Indian Ocean. We had more than six thousand miles to navigate across this ocean body before seeing land again. Then, we would reach the Pacific Ocean at the southern part of the Australian continent, and turn northeast toward the ports of Sydney and then Newport.

The Indian Ocean waters were fortunately calm since we were sailing during the months between the tropical cyclone seasons of the northern and southern regions of this ocean. Salty ocean-spray continuously filled the air, and the steady wind currents carried the *Fennia* with ease across the diamond-sparkling waters. Multiple pods of dolphins trailed alongside the ship. Energetically, they would leap from the water and perform their acrobatics in the air. Their happy squeaking noises and splashes back into the water were amusing sights to watch, helping to break the monotony of each day's sameness upon the ocean. The unrelenting beating of the ship's sails had become commonplace to my ears. The rhythmic rocking and pitching of the ship had become an unobserved normalcy.

Meals were regularly prepared and eaten and cleaned up afterwards. The telescope constantly scanned the surrounding waters for ships that might be of danger to us.

During the long traverse across the Indian Ocean, I spent time with my Bible, reading about Jesus' life recorded in the Gospels. One story that fascinated me was when He fell asleep in the boat while a turbulent storm hit and threatened the lives of those on board. Amidst the peril, He was able to sleep. I wondered about that kind of serenity. It personally gave me another outcome to hope for—of having an inner quietude despite any circumstance. Currently, our peril wasn't the stormy seas but the dangers imposed by war upon the seas. And so, I imagined that my Friend was on board the *Fennia*, sleeping calmly through our imagined terrors.

It was my twenty-third birthday, November 4, when we finally sailed into the port of Sydney, ending the long days we had been at sea. In Sydney we learned that grave concern had been present as to where the remaining five-cruiser German squadron had been hiding out since leaving the coast of China when Japan entered the war. Eight of the thirteen German cruisers that had been in foreign waters when the war began in August had already been incapacitated. After the Royal Navy and the Japanese had spent months searching for the remaining five-cruiser squadron, a radio communication on September 26 had been intercepted which confirmed the German squadron's intent of targeting the merchant ships coming and going from major trading routes along the west coast of South America.

The British fleet tracking them, which was only four ships strong, assembled together and by October 22 was stationed off the coast of the Falkland Islands. Upon further learning that the German squadron was off the coast of central Chile, the British fleet was determined to destroy the German squadron. Due to some miscommunication with London and the delay of reinforcements, the fleet chose to advance toward the Chilean coastline to the port of Coronel via Cape Horn and get ready to do battle.

The German squadron received word of the British fleet's presence in Coronel. They had been hiding out at the Chilean port of Valparaiso, which was just north of the port of Talca, our next destination after leaving Australia. All five German cruisers immediately left the port of Valparaiso and headed south to meet the British fleet. On the evening of November 1, the British fleet found itself confronting the German squadron in very difficult seas, mostly to British disadvantage. Unfortunately, they were no match for the superiority of the German squadron's positioning, and two of the four British ships were sunk. The other two ships escaped back to the Falkland Islands with damages. Before midnight that night, another sixteen hundred seamen had been killed on those two British ships—forever lost as more casualties of war.

Consternation was again nagging at our souls from this newest information we had learned while in the port of Sydney. However, we had another destination to reach with our cargo. Waiting wouldn't prove to be prudent and instead might prove more detrimental. And so, our captain gave orders to set sail for Talca in Chile, not knowing that on November 11 the British Admiralty in London had sent two battlecruisers from the Grand Fleet to hunt and destroy the German squadron. The battlecruisers had left Plymouth while other fleets of ships were being sent to band together at strategic points in the South Atlantic and Pacific Oceans to block the German squadron from escape.

This voyage had become long, much longer than I had anticipated it to be. Somehow the tensions of war contributed to an anxious state that often made time seem to drag even slower. I struggled to hold on to hope for a positive outcome of this voyage. Already three months had passed, most of the time seeing seemingly infinite miles of ocean. Now, as the *Fennia* left the harbor of Newcastle in Australia, we faced more than eight thousand miles until we would reach the port of Talca in Chile, hoping to not encounter the rogue German squadron.

The Pacific Ocean is the world's largest ocean and covers one-third of the earth's surface. It is even larger than all of the masses of land on the earth put together. Its name means "peaceful sea," and for the most part, we found that to be true. However, the closer to Chile we came, the more unpredictable the weather became—and the seas wilder. We began to encounter the effects of the division of the South Equatorial Current where one branch flows around Cape Horn and the other turns northward along the Chilean coast, making it difficult to navigate the seas. With the skill of our captain and crew, we did arrive safely at the port of Talca in Chile the week before Christmas. Here we learned the rest of the story about the German squadron being pursued.

Feeling elated with their victory at Coronel, the German squadron had returned to the port of Valparaiso. But their triumph soon turned to fear and indecision regarding what to do next. Wanting to return home because they had used up almost half of the squadron's major-caliber ammunition, and knowing they were ten thousand miles from home, they feared this might not be possible. They were also fearful that the powerful British Navy would retaliate because of their severe losses imposed at Coronel, thus making it home might prove to be a risky challenge.

The two British battlecruisers, previously deployed from the Grand Fleet, had been concentrating their operation at Abrolhos Rocks off the coast of Brazil. On November 26 they began to head south to the Falkland Islands—the very same day the German squadron left St. Quintin Bay in the archipelagic maze off the southern Chilean coast where they had been hiding out and stalling for time.

It was the summer season in these latitudes, and summer weather was most often atrocious on these ocean waters. The German squadron, anticipating calmer winds, had waited until midnight of December 1 to go around Cape Horn and then sail up to the Falkland Islands. From there, they hoped to make a run for home across the Atlantic Ocean. On December 8 they arrived at the Falkland Islands with the intent of destroying the wireless communication station at Port Stanley. However, to their surprise their ships began to receive enemy fire. Turning their ships eastward, they tried to outrun the British who had arrived the day before at Port Stanley. Four of the five German cruisers were sunk off the coast of the Falkland Islands that day by the British. Only one cruiser got away.

The *Fennia* had escaped a major threat that had been haunting us since we had left Australia. The hostilities involving this major threat were finally eliminated just one week ahead of our scheduled port arrival at Talca. There was still one wild card of the German squadron that remained, which posed a threat to us and other sailing merchant ships; however, its whereabouts remained unknown.

And so, after Christmas, when our business was completed in Talca, the *Fennia* prepared itself for the ten thousand mile voyage back to northern Europe. The captain's spirits were lighter, knowing that there was only one menacing ship to be on the watch for, instead of five. But he was also aware of the terrors one could encounter while passing around Cape Horn through the Drake Passage. The story of the *Edward Sewall*, a four-mast vessel, and its voyage around the Cape in the spring of 1904 was one our captain knew about. It took the *Edward Sewall* fifty-nine harrowing days to navigate the Drake Passage in a westerly direction. We would be navigating it in an easterly direction.

The terrible Drake Passage is a violent area of water on this earth's surface. It is a very complicated passage of water that lies between the continents of South America and Antarctica and is a span of water four hundred miles wide. There is an area sixty miles wide for ships to pass through between the land masses of Cape Horn, an island at the southern tip of Chile, and the Diego Ramirez Islands further out into the Drake Passage.

One very intimidating complication of the Drake Passage is the Antarctic Circumpolar Current. This current carries a huge volume of water that flows about six hundred times the transport of the Amazon River. This tremendous flow of water travels eastward unimpeded by any significant land masses as it travels through the Drake Passage and around Antarctica. Waves more than thirty-two feet high are not unusual and can be more than sixty-five feet high when the Antarctic's strong wind gales are blowing across the passage. Wind gales blow over two hundred days of the year, and the rest of the year the wind is strong. There are more than one hundred thirty days of cloudy skies, sometimes accompanied by fog.

The latitudinal positioning of this passage of water, located between 56 degrees south at Cape Horn and 60 degrees south at the Shetland Islands off the coast of Antarctica, gave rise to the old sailor's adage: "Below 40 degrees, there is no law; below 50 degrees, there is no God."

One naturally feels disturbed and anxious when approaching this hostile and portentous passage that frightfully allows ships to leave the Pacific Ocean and enter the Atlantic Ocean, or vice versa, at the place where the earth's 60 degree meridian intersects the passage. The unexpected can worsen in a very short time.

And so, with these formidable odds, we took on the challenge of the Drake Passage. Rounding Cape Horn was considered completed only after traversing the one thousand mile stretch from Wellington along the south Chilean coast over to the Falkland Islands off the south coast of Argentina. With only two hundred miles to sail before entering this dreadful arc, we left Talca's port and braced ourselves as well as we could for whatever would happen in the rough waters ahead. The captain maintained his trust in the skills of his crew and his vessel. He knew that the *Fennia* was a sturdy ship, for Finland was known for its craft in building seaworthy vessels.

I remember sitting on the bed in my sleeping quarters and looking at the picture of my sweetheart, hopeful that I would see her in just a few weeks. I thought of my family members in Finland and wondered how their lives had fared over the last months. I thought of Pauli in his new country. I was grateful that our food supply was holding out well on board even though the weather had been very warm since leaving Europe.

I took out my Bible and read one of my Friend's promises. It said, "Let not your heart be troubled: ye believe in God, believe also in me."[3] Again, I pictured my Friend aboard the *Fennia* sleeping soundly. My shipmates were very wary about the winds and waters ahead. Even though my concerns were high, I chose to hope in an unbeaten passage to the Atlantic Ocean, which would take us home.

A few days later dawn broke the horizon ahead, revealing choppy water as we made our way into the Drake Passage. The square-rigged sails shuddered as strong winds ripped between them. Breakfast had been served early so that extra vigilance on deck would be possible. I remember going on deck after cleaning the eating area. Beginning to appear in the distance I could see the jagged rocks of Cape Horn's face, which rises fourteen hundred feet above the water. Albatrosses lazily moved their wings as they glided above the water, watching for the moment in which to dive in to catch a fish. They appeared so unconcerned about the treacherous geography in which they lived their lives. Once or twice we spotted a pod of whales blowing water straight into the air. They seemed to enjoy the cold, vicious water currents of the Antarctic. Everything felt surreal about the nature around us.

The sun was rising fast in the sky. As we neared Cape Horn, a fog began to surround the ship. Within the hour,

---

3   John 14:1 (KJV)

the ship began pitching and listing dramatically against the waves. Soon, the swaying of the ship became enormous. Roaring waves crashed against the ship's hull, their power unimaginable. The angry water had turned into a frothy-white, swirling mass below the ship. Winds began howling and screaming. The noise was deafening. The captain ordered all nonessential crew to be confined below the ship's deck for safety and to rest as much as was possible so they could relieve those who remained on deck.

By noon, dense fog allowed no light from the sun to be seen above us. Unmercifully, the strong currents and building wind gales tossed the *Fennia* like a cork on the water. This torment persisted into the next day and the next; for days the ship floundered amongst the colossal waves that had begun to wash aboard the ship's deck. Fog persisted day and night, and it felt like we had entered an unending abyss of terror.

Gallantly, the crew rotated above and below decks, working tirelessly to keep the ship upright. Everyone on board was soaked from the raging waves. I did my best to keep the crew fed; however, everyone was experiencing intense seasickness from the radical motion of the ship. All was in chaos.

Day after day this writhing storm pounded our ship. The captain began to give orders to throw overboard anything not absolutely necessary for our survival to lighten the ship's weight. Many of the traded goods we were returning to England had to go overboard. We held on to our food supplies, but much of them was fast becoming unusable from being damaged in the storm. I carefully guarded the flour and drinking water, keeping those items as safe as possible.

Men were beginning to get ill from being wet and cold. The captain asked me to care for a very sick shipmate in the forecastle of the ship where the crew's sleeping quarters were located. One day I was responding to orders up on the ship's deck in-between caring for my shipmate. No sooner had I entered the deck when a mountainous wave swept me off the ship just as it listed toward the sea. And then, just as rapidly, another wave responded by placing me back on the deck of the ship just as the ship was listing in the opposite direction, slamming me against one of the ship's masts.

I was greatly dazed by this event and returned below deck to check on my sick shipmate and also stop myself from violently shaking, both from fright and from the icy waters that had almost become my grave. I knew I was badly bruised from hitting the mast, but I was so thankful it had been there to stop me. Entering the forecastle, I noted that the very sick man was asleep, so I went to my quarters, dripping wet and hardly able to stand upright from the pitching of the ship.

My first thought was to make sure my Bible hadn't been lost in the pounding storm. Grateful that it was dry and safely in its place, I sank to my knees and, with tears, thanked my Friend for saving my life. I told Him that I was sorry for my doubts, which were so overwhelming to me. I asked Him to help me find strength to bear the torment of this storm. Just talking to Him calmed my anguish. I was still soaking wet, the storm was still raging, but I felt a quietness inside begin to push away the troubling fears.

The next day my sick shipmate died. I helped to put him into a canvass sack. We weighted the sack and helplessly thrust him overboard. I brought the captain his *Book of*

Common Prayers, and he read the words out loud to those of us on deck, "From dust thou art, and unto dust shalt thou return, and our Lord Jesus Christ shall raise you in the last day." Tears were in the eyes of my sea-hardened shipmates, and tears also fell down my cheeks as we all struggled to stand upright safely on the deck and simultaneously deal with our grief. We had all tragically lost a comrade.

According to the logs the captain kept, this storm raged for three weeks. Finally, it mercifully subsided. The sturdy *Fennia* had valiantly weathered its beating. When the skies cleared and the waters settled, the captain was able to read the compass and determine where we had ended up. The strong currents had carried us into the Scotia Sea three hundred miles north of King George Island, which is off the coast of Antarctica. Now, finally, we could begin to chart our course back up the Atlantic Ocean and sail the rest of the ten thousand miles home.

One day, while everyone on board was aching to get home, the ship's second mate found me. He had been best friend to the man who had died and whom we had to thrust overboard into the wild ocean. He wanted to thank me for doing my best to keep his friend alive. As we talked, he told me that up until that day he hadn't believed there was a God. After the prayer words had been read aloud by the captain as a memorial to his friend, he began to change his thinking about God. By the time we finished our talk, I was able to share with him how God and His Son had always been my friends in life. And before we reached the coastlines of Europe, the second mate had begun to understand that there was a loving God who deeply cared about people on this earth—including him.

The storm had taken its toll on our food supply. The remains of our two-year supply had all but vanished, having been damaged or destroyed by the storm. For the last two weeks of the voyage to Europe, all I had was flour, water, and baking powder in which to make biscuits to feed the crew. Somehow, the supply lasted until we returned home. No one complained. Our stomachs did not experience the discomfort of hunger; warm biscuits kept the discomfort away. The good news was that we were all alive, and what a story we had to tell. To this day, I'm not fond of eating baking powder biscuits, but I sure learned how to make them, even with some of the usual ingredients missing.

It was late March 1915 when our weary crew and food-depleted *Fennia* sailed into the port of Dunkirk, France. We learned that the last German cruiser which had haunted our travels home had just been sunk by the British on March 14 in the Juan Fernandez Islands—about three hundred sixty miles west of Valparaiso, Chile. In the first seven months of the war, Germany's sea power had been fatally crippled and cleared from the outer oceans by the British Navy and its allies. Germany's oceanic trade had come to a halt and her own port approaches were tightly barricaded by British Navy blockades. The waters surrounding all of Europe's coastlines were heavily guarded. We were almost home, however, nothing was ever the same again.

Hope had succeeded in rewarding my desires of a successful future. It had succeeded in calming my fears. It had given me strength to endure peril and anxieties. During those years on the great oceans, I had experienced a tangled mixture of wonder and dread. I had learned that life was adventurous

The Songs

and also that it was no trivial matter. Most of all, I learned that I always had my Friend with me, my Friend who had become the Lord of the water for me.

While one may think He sometimes is sleeping, His eyes are watching and His arms of protection are always present. These two songs remind me of my voyages upon the great oceans and seas.

Master, the tempest is raging!

The billows are tossing high!

The sky is o'er shadowed with blackness;

No shelter or help is nigh;

Carest Thou not that we perish?

How canst Thou lie asleep,

When each moment so madly is threatening

A grave in the angry deep?

Master, with anguish of spirit

I bow in my grief today;

The depths of my sad heart are troubled;

O, waken and save, I pray!

Torrents of sin and of anguish

Sweep o'er my sinking soul;

And I perish! I perish! Dear Master;

O hasten, and take control.

Master, the terror is over,

The elements sweetly rest;

Earth's sun in the calm lake is mirrored;

And heaven's within my breast;

Linger, O blessed Redeemer,

Leave me alone no more;

And with joy I shall make the blest harbor,

And rest on the blissful shore.

The winds and the waves

Shall obey My will, peace, be still!

The Songs

Whether the wrath of the storm-tossed sea,

Or demons, or men, or whatever it be,

No water can swallow the ship where lies

The Master of ocean, and earth, and skies;

They all shall sweetly obey My will;

Peace, be still, Peace, be still!

They all shall sweetly obey My will;

Peace, peace, be still![4]

~~~~~~

Jesus, Savior, pilot me

Over life's tempestuous sea;

Unknown waves before me roll,

Hiding rock and treacherous shoal;

Chart and compass come from Thee;

Jesus, Savior, pilot me.

---

4   M. A. Baker, "Peace Be Still," (1874).

As a mother stills her child,

Thou canst hush the ocean wild;

Boisterous waves obey Thy will,

When Thou sayest to them, "Be still!"

Wondrous Sovereign of the sea,

Jesus, Savior, pilot me.

When at last I near the shore,

And the fearful breakers roar

'Twixt me and the peaceful rest,

Then, while leaning on Thy breast,

May I hear Thee say to me,

"Fear not, I will pilot thee."[5]

---

5   Edward Hopper, "Jesus, Savior, Pilot Me," (1871).

My Story

When I reflect back on Grandpa's stories of ships and oceans and distant shores, I have learned to realize that hope matters. It directs the course of one's life toward meaningful goals. It lightens burdens and casts a glimmer on hoped for desires. It provides the way to be patient while circumstances and directions unfold. Hope is a gift to cherish, for without it, we would miss experiencing our longed for destination, because we wouldn't be able to recognize its arrival.

"I led them with cords of human kindness, with ties of love." Hosea 11:4

Love

Grandpa's Story

I wasn't able to make it back to Finland from France. Our merchant trading voyages for Finland had ended with the escalating war. England had imposed a naval blockade around Germany in the North Sea. The Russian fleet was busy staving off German ships in the Baltic Sea. These blockades had enraged the Germans, and in February 1915 Germany had declared the waters around the British Isles a war zone. To retaliate, the Germans began laying mines in these waters. These mine fields and the prowling German submarines had become the new menace of the sea. This caused dangerous threats for all ships. Most merchant ships, now acting as naval merchant ships, were actively engaged in transporting war materials for the Allied Powers.

By the time the *Fennia* had returned to the French port of Dunkirk in March 1915, we were told that eighty-six allied ships had already been sunk since February by the mine and submarine attacks of the Germans. Airplane escorts were sometimes helpful in being able to spot the approaching submarines; however, the naval merchant ships began to travel in convoys for extra protection. The waters had become a death-defying risk to traverse.

In the battlefields on land, the horrific use of artillery and poison gasses were extinguishing thousands and thousands of lives. In April we learned that the Germans had used chlorine gas for the first time in the trenches of the Allies, wildly rising fears among the troops while the death tolls climbed higher.

What choice was I to make now? My health was somewhat weakened from the lack of nutrition and exposure to the elements from our passage around Cape Horn. My career as steward had abruptly ended. I had no training as a soldier. I couldn't get home to Finland, and I desperately wondered how my family members were doing in my homeland.

Many of my shipmates decided to join up with the naval merchant ships. These ships were taking incredible risks for the Allied Powers by transporting war materials, troops, fuel, and ammunition to the many areas where these were critically needed or being acquired. Sometimes the naval merchant ships would assist the troops in either evacuating or landing. Feeling compelled to help win this awful war, I decided I would join up with the mission of these dedicated ships. And so, I left the *Fennia* after it docked in the port of Bristol, England. Our captain was making plans with the British to use the *Fennia* as one of the allied naval merchant ships. It made me sad to tell the *Fennia's* captain good-bye. He had been very good to me, and my loyalty to him was strong. In the meantime, I found a ship I could immediately join in the war efforts.

The first ship I volunteered on was heavily loaded with dynamite and ammunitions to be taken to LeHavre, France. Because the naval merchant ships were traveling in convoys, maneuvering the ships in the mine-infested waters at times became harrowing. We left the port of Bristol and began to assemble into a convoy formation. The ships were of different sizes, and the waters of the Bristol Channel were tight. There were seven ships in our convoy, each carrying different materials to France. Tensions about safe transport through the waters were high as the ships collaborated to reach formation for travel together.

The ship I was on was one of the outermost ships in the convoy and nearest to England's coastline. No sooner had we assembled safely into a convoy and were carefully moving out of the Bristol Channel when a passenger ship was spotted looming in front of us—directly progressing toward the ship I was on. The first mate immediately hoisted red lights on the ship's mast and began to ring the bell to warn the ship of its danger. I had been asleep, trying to catch up on some much needed rest when I heard the commotion, which awakened me.

Frantically, one of the crew members ran through the ship warning everyone that the ship was on a collision course with another ship. I hurried up to the deck and found myself staring at the hull of an enormous passenger ship bearing the Canadian flag. Its decks were lined with soldiers in uniform, arriving from Canada to help England fight for victory against the Central Powers.

Earnestly, I began to pray to my Friend to spare the lives of both crews and keep our ships safe. There was nothing to do after that but wait for the impending impact, or a miracle to happen. In only minutes, the passenger ship slid by our ship within two feet of it. I could have reached out and touched its sides—it was that close. All held their breath as the two ships precariously glided by each other without a scratch.

The crews of both ships broke out with cheering, and the heightened tensions evaporated with blessed relief when the crisis was past. Silently, I thanked my Friend for protecting me and everyone involved from disaster upon the sea. He was Lord of the sea, and my heart turned toward Him with tender affection and deep gratitude. Why was He so interested in keeping my life protected? I deeply wondered about that, especially when daily so many others around me were losing their lives in the war.

Returning to England from the French port of LeHavre, our ship—now empty of ammunitions—carried injured troops back to England for care. The sights and sounds of the injured were pitiful, and my heart ached for them as we loaded their battered bodies onto the ship and tried to keep them as comfortable as possible. Many died before we reached the shores of England. As we traversed the war-contaminated waters, we had no assurance of being able to survive a torpedo attack by submarines skulking below. But we pressed on with our determined goal of the necessary transportation that war demanded. There were five ships in the convoy returning along with ours back to England, most carrying dead and injured soldiers.

The convoy of ships safely arrived back to the port of Bristol. After helping to empty our ship of the dead and wounded, I caught the next available train and went to

Maryport, a British port along the northern edge of the Irish Sea. Here I was to join the crew of the naval merchant ship *Polwell*, a steamship loaded with mustard gas to be taken to France. The *Polwell* would then sail for San Francisco to load up with ammunition to bring back to England. I had volunteered to be the cook on board to feed the crew of this armed ship. Knowing that we were scheduled to pass through the newly opened Panama Canal, my fears were allayed about taking this trip on the open oceans to America. We would not have to deal with Cape Horn and the dreadful Drake Passage. Also, the voyage would not take as long, for the steam-powered vessel would move much faster than the sailing ships I was used to.

During this period, I began to lose all sense of time. Balancing stress and optimism became a complicated challenge for me. Changes were happening in my life so rapidly. I was having to adjust to many new and difficult realities. My passport was no longer a necessary document for travel, and the rules and regulations of the ports had been changed because of war. I was no longer a ship's officer. Only the Royal Naval ships retained rank determinations. With the exception of the captain and first mate, most of the naval merchant ship crews consisted of a hodgepodge of older men and very young men—some only fifteen years old. They were usually volunteers—most did not have any formal training regarding ship duties or uniforms to identify themselves. But they were loyal and tenacious in supporting the war efforts and each other. I did my best as the volunteer cook to build camaraderie with the new crew I had joined.

My pay had been terminated because the *Fennia* had

become a naval merchant ship for the British Admiralty when it returned to Europe, as were other Finnish ships that had remained outside of the Baltic Sea since the war's beginning. Usually, our pay was dependent upon approval by the Russian government. Since the *Fennia* never made it back to Finland, we could not collect our pay for our last voyage to Australia and South America. We were promised that compensation would come but that it would take time. The only money I had was a few coins jingling in my pockets. I was virtually penniless.

I definitely was anxious about the hazardous cargo of poisonous mustard gas we were transporting to France. This was a lethal combination with the possible torpedo and mine attacks that threatened us every day. The risks were exceedingly high. Even so, I did my best to keep our determined crew heartily fed with the food supplies we were given by the Royal Navy. The galley was the only place where I didn't feel displaced and uneasy. I was grateful for this one haven, even though I also helped out with other duties on board the *Polwell*.

I remember wondering how I would be able to cope with the myriad of fragmentations that were invading my life if I didn't have faith and hope as anchors. I couldn't imagine how very desperate all would appear to be without faith and hope—especially during the hours it took to travel the length of the Irish Sea and back through the English Channel and on to the French port of LeHavre to deliver the venomous mustard gas. The gravity of being on the verge of dying at any moment became a taxing burden to bear, and faith and hope were there to give me confidence instead of insanity. My

Friend was aboard—I was certain of that.

Even though I had lost track of time, I knew that summer was well underway, for the air temperatures offered indication of its arrival. The hot, humid air hung in a haze about us, but its discomfort was nothing when compared to the uneasiness of transporting hazardous supplies in tainted waters. Once the *Polwell* was able to begin heading west across the Atlantic Ocean, most of the tormenting concerns were relieved. The *Polwell* was basically empty of cargo when we left France so that we could load the needed ammunitions in San Francisco. This made our steam-powered travels much faster upon the ocean. Actually, being empty greatly benefited us by saving time in traversing the Atlantic Ocean, because we ended up losing some days when we reached the Panama Canal.

Passing through the waters of the Caribbean brought back memories of days that now seemed so long ago. As the *Polwell* steamed through the Caribbean, I again caught glimpses of the balmy islands that had made previous winters so enjoyable to me. After passing by the islands, it didn't take long before we arrived at the Panama Canal—ready to make the forty-eight mile transition through the series of locks that would allow us to leave the Atlantic Ocean and enter the Pacific Ocean.

Announcements of the long-awaited opening of the Panama Canal in August 1914 had been overshadowed by the major news flooding the presses regarding the Great War. The engineering and building of the canal was one of the world's greatest feats ever undertaken, but the news of its opening was relegated to the back pages of newspapers while the events of the war continued to unfold and be foremost as the stories making the headlines.

Since its opening, the Panama Canal had been successfully used by ships traveling from New York to San Francisco, reducing their voyage lengths from fourteen thousand miles via Cape Horn to only six thousand miles. Now, as the Great War advanced, allied ships were beginning to make efficient use of the canal. I was looking forward to passing through the Panama Canal. For me, it was an intriguing event to be able to experience and a high point of this voyage.

As our ship came upon the canal, we waited in line to be given the go ahead for entering the series of locks. Unfortunately, the locks were experiencing technical difficulties, so we had to wait for the problem to be fixed. After waiting for almost two weeks, our ship's turn came to enter the canal. All went well until about halfway through when the second set of locks wouldn't work properly. The *Polwell* was stuck and had to wait another two days until the locks were back working and we could complete the passage. The officials at the canal gave us advanced warning that if the *Polwell* would be returning through the canal within the next three weeks, the ship would not be able to get through. The canal was being closed for repairs to fix the problems currently being encountered with the locks.

And so, up the Pacific Ocean to San Francisco the *Polwell* steamed, arriving in the port on September 12, 1915—a date I will forever remember because I had some decisions to make. It was a very clear day, and the sites of the beautiful tree-laden shorelines caught my attention as we entered the San Francisco Bay waters. Our turnaround time in San Francisco to load ammunitions was to be relatively short—much shorter than the time remaining before the Panama Canal would again be open for use. Our captain was determined to get the ammunitions back to England without further delays. England needed the ammunitions.

I kept close to the ship, intending to learn if we would be waiting until the Panama Canal was again open or if we would be returning to Europe around Cape Horn with our load of ammunitions. I was beside myself with consternation as I remembered the terrifying passage around Cape Horn only nine months earlier. I could not bring myself to even imagine crossing those ill-fated waters ever again. I felt my stomach become nauseous and my legs become weak as I wrestled with the possibility of having to traverse the Drake Passage.

Emotionally, the fear was too much for me to ever bear experiencing again. The memories of the *Fennia* diving mercilessly into the deep trenches of the massive waves after being forced to crest their dangerous peaks, of the screaming winds that raged and tossed us about for three weeks, of the vomit, debris, illness, and chaos that plagued our ship—all these thoughts made me instantly relive the terror and panic of that storm. I vowed to myself that I would leave the *Polwell* before I would submit to the terror of the waters around Cape Horn. Waiting to hear the captain's final decision was a very anxious time for me.

I had finished serving the noon meal one day when our crew was given confirmation by the captain that the *Polwell* was to leave San Francisco in two days and return via Cape Horn. After cleaning up the galley, I very quietly assembled the meager belongings that were mine and carefully hid them on my person so they wouldn't be noticed. With very little food and a few coins in my pocket, not of U.S. currency, I left the *Polwell* and walked to the city streets of San Francisco to decide on a plan of action.

The celebrations of the Panama-Pacific International Exposition had begun in February of that year and were still underway in September when the *Polwell* arrived in San Francisco. Congress had chosen San Francisco to be the city to host this exposition in 1915, which was celebrating the newly opened Panama Canal and also was commemorating the discovery of the Pacific Ocean four hundred years earlier by the Spanish explorer Balboa. In hopes of showing the world that San Francisco had recovered from the destructive earthquake and subsequent fires that had hit in 1906, the city was thrilled to be chosen to herald the innovative technologies of the future being featured in the extravagant exhibits built by many U.S. states and thirty-one countries of the world.

From the port of San Francisco, one couldn't miss the displays of lights and the grandly built exhibits. The grandeur was exceptional, and it was apparent that many visitors were still flooding to San Francisco for this stunning event. The walkways of the exposition were crowded and bustling day and night. And so, because of my plan to leave the *Polwell*, I anonymously became one of the supposed visitors of the exposition while blending in with the crowds.

After inconspicuously mingling around in the crowds for about an hour, I came across a man who was speaking Swedish. I couldn't speak English, so I relied on Swedish, my second language, for communicating with this man. Making small talk with him, I learned that visitors were typically paying one dollar per day for a hotel room, and meals were costing another dollar per day. He had traveled from New York

City to the exposition and had been enjoying San Francisco for the past week. He made sure to tell me which exhibits to definitely visit, and he pointed out the hotel where he had been staying and its close proximity to the exposition grounds. I appreciated the information I had gleaned from him, and after wishing him well, I continued on through the crowds. The afternoon hours began to slip away; however, my mind was hustling to devise and refine a plan of action.

It soon became clear to me that staying inside the exposition areas would probably make it easier for the ship's crew to find me. Because I had no money, I couldn't pay for a hotel room in which to hide, let alone buy any food. I couldn't just keep mingling in the exposition crowds for the next few days without the probability of being noticed by someone from our ship who would be out looking for me. I knew the crew would try hard to find me, for they had become my friends. Then I would be forced to leave with the ship and have no chance to escape.

Casually, but with an unwavering resolve to keep on walking, I strolled on through the marvelous walkways of the exquisite exposition, wondering with amazement at the structures and lights that covered more than six hundred thirty acres of land along the northern shoreline of San Francisco. Knowing that I had only two days—the rest of that day and the next—to find a place to hide out, I opted to just keep going west after I eventually left the perimeter of the exposition. My memory vividly reminded me about the dense trees and hilly areas along the coastline that I had noticed as the *Polwell* was rounding Fort Point while making its way east to the port of San Francisco when we had arrived two days previously.

The trees looked so different from the trees along Finland's coastline, which I had found interesting.

With the dazzle and crowds of the exposition drifting farther behind me, I knew I was safer, but I kept walking, surveying the secluded landscape along the coastline until I no longer saw a human being. Then, carefully, I began to climb the incline of the steep, craggy hills that were heavily wooded with dark green trees. The earthy smell of damp dirt wafted across the balmy September air, and the ground was soft and quiet as my feet kept on moving upon it. The light from the sun became less and less visible while I ventured deeper into the tree-laden hillside, trying to find a place of shelter where I could hide and wait. I noticed different kinds of wild berries sprinkled here and there along the way—especially the laurel berries—and was pleased to see them, for I had carried very little food with me.

Finding a cave-like indentation among the boulders and brambles of the secluded hillside, I chose to make this my haven for the next five days. I found a sturdy stick and notched out a chunk with my pocketknife to mark that the first day was accounted for. Then, each day afterwards I planned to notch out another chunk when I could see sunlight filtering in through the trees. In this way I would know how many days had passed by. I was certain that the *Polwell* would be on its way back to England within five days—even if they couldn't locate me. I didn't dare lose track of time.

Night eventually descended upon the hills, bringing with it complete darkness. A coolness permeated the air as it rolled off the Pacific Ocean amidst a thin mist of fog. I was thankful for the recesses of the cave I had found, for it helped keep me warm. There was nothing to do but wait, think, rest, and hope beyond all resolve that no one would find me. That first night I fell into a fitful sleep that kept me tossing with fractured thoughts and fears.

I awoke early the following morning. The sunlight was barely visible from above the treetops. Birds were singing their happy morning songs from within the tree branches around me. Crawling out of the safety of the cave, I stood up and stretched out the kinks in my body. Although I had covered the hard ground with branches and leaves before night had arrived, it had offered little padding from the hard ground. I was safe but unwilling to give in to feeling too much relief. There were still four days ahead to be concerned about. I opened my pocketknife and made the second notch in my stick.

It was fear that was driving me to abandon the *Polwell,* and I felt as if I was living in a nightmare. Was I wrong in becoming a fugitive? Was I being cowardly, or being practical about my safety? Why was it so difficult to deal with the strain that fear had left imprinted upon me by Cape Horn? Was I just worn down by all of the nagging stresses that had been plaguing my life since the Great War had begun over a year ago? How does one ever understand the changes that war imposes on societies and individual lives? What would I do once the *Polwell* was gone from San Francisco? Would any official in America ever understand my situation? How would I learn to speak English? Where would I live and find work? What would I tell my family—my sweetheart—my friends? What would this decision mean for my future and being able to return to Finland someday?

I felt so alone—so discouraged—so unsure about everything except my escape from re-living the known terrors of Cape Horn. I was torn between my great fear and the humility of facing its consequences. Guilt for surrendering so completely to real, intimidating fear riddled my soul. I had always been a responsible person—now, I was doubting my own inner resources. How would I turn this around in an honest way in order for my future to be lived without remorse? On and on, the endless thoughts and questions tumbled around in my head.

On that second day, when enough light filtered in through the trees to be able to read, I took my Bible out from the pocket where I was safely carrying it. Knowing I needed help from outside of myself, I chose again to read the Gospel of John. I had found comfort there before, and I still had enough real faith that my Friend would give me help and direction through this perplexing situation. He had never abandoned me before. This gave me hope for a solution.

I began to read my Friend's words: "My Father, which gave them me, is greater than all; and no man is able to pluck them out of my Father's hand."[6] "For the Father himself loveth you, because ye have loved me, and have believed that I came out from God.... These things I have spoken unto you, that in me ye might have peace. In the world ye shall have tribulation: but be of good cheer; I have overcome the world."[7]

And so, with a distraught heart bleeding with despair and desired hope, I lowered myself upon the decomposing elements covering the ground—ground which at that moment was hallowed to me—and asked my Friend for help and

6   John 10:29 (KJV)
7   John 16:27, 33 (KJV)

peace. Trusting was the only option I had, and I resolutely hung onto it. I would continue to do my part and watch for a solution to unfold. With this new determination and support from my Friend, I felt the heavy burdens beginning to lift and peace filtering softly across my troubled heart.

My food supply was very scanty, and I was stretching it as far as I could, but I was becoming quite hungry. By staying in and around the cave, I knew I would expend less energy. In the evening hours just before sundown, I returned to the areas where I had seen wild berries, which helped to keep my hunger satiated. As each of the five days passed by uneventfully, the panic that had had its stranglehold on me began to subside. I didn't see the *Polwell* move back through the waters around Fort Point and into the open Pacific Ocean because I was tucked away amidst the dense trees in the landscape of the shoreline the day that the ship passed by me.

The morning I made the fifth notch on my stick, I decided to wait until mid-afternoon to begin making my way back to the crowds and noises of the exposition and then cautiously check the port for myself to make sure the *Polwell* was gone. After that, I would find a way to get bathed and cleaned up and locate someone who could speak Finnish or Swedish. It felt good to have a plan, and I was energized to carry it through, even though I had no idea of the particulars I would encounter, nor of how I would get some food, for I was so very hungry—and feeling quite weak.

I began working my way back down the hillside to where I had a view of the Pacific Ocean, picking and eating the last handfuls of berries I could find to help ease my hunger. From the position of the sun in the sky, I was sure it was mid-afternoon. For a few minutes, I sat down on the ground and let the sea-breeze blow over me. It felt so refreshing. Sea gulls were gliding along the shore above the ocean water. Seeing the bright light in the sky, which also bounced off the ocean, made my eyes squint. They were accustomed to the dimness of the light surrounding the maze of trees that had kept me safe. I felt kind of exposed—like a bug that had just crawled out from living under a rock for the past five days.

While my body adjusted to being out in the open air and light, I began pulling together my inner resources for the adventures ahead while again thanking my Friend for His love toward me—a fugitive in another country. Then I remembered His long visit to the earth—a country far away from His Father in heaven. At that moment, I knew my Friend understood what feeling alone in another country was like. Because of that, I knew I could find solitude in His strength to persevere. I was humbled by the undeserved compassion my Friend kept having for me. My heart reached out to Him with deep gratitude. I wished I could fall at His feet and thank Him and ask Him why He cared so much about my life. Who was I that I deserved such continued favor from Him? Being unable to answer those questions, I just trusted in the reality of His love continually being shown to me. Maybe someday I would find the answer. I chose to hope for finding that answer one day.

It was approximately a three mile walk to get back to the port. Walking felt good, and the freedom of again being in open spaces was invigorating. I was very hungry and thirsty, so my energy was at lean levels. The day before I had swallowed the last of the water I had carried with me. My food supply had been gone for three days. Fortunately, the weather wasn't very hot, and so I pressed on.

Within the hour I was back inside the boundaries of the exposition. The smells of food weren't hard for me to miss. Feeling a bit self-conscious about how I must look after the past five days, I pulled on my woolen beret-cap and tried to be inconspicuous among the crowds of people. I walked, mostly looking down, to avoid much eye contact. To my surprise, I happened to notice a crumpled dollar bill laying on the walkway in front of me. I bent down to pick it up and found myself holding my first American money. This was definitely a gift from my Friend—for that I was certain.

Another thirty minutes of walking got me back to the port where I scanned each of the perpendicular docks jutting out into the ocean to see if the *Polwell* was still there. She was gone. Both profound relief and a resolve to succeed in my new circumstances collided within me. Turning away from the docks, I stopped to evaluate how I would proceed in finding a place to get cleaned up and to find food.

In the shadows of one of the walkways that connected the docks, I caught a gleam of light shining off of a coin. Scattered near it were four more coins. I stooped to pick them up, saying a prayer of thanks for this second gift of money. Now I would be able to find a hotel for one night and eat a meal. Tears filled my eyes, and I reached up and wiped them away with the back of my hand. Not only had my Friend fed crowds of people with two loaves of bread and five fish while in Galilee, but He was feeding and caring for me right now. It wasn't the miracle that astounded me; it was the reason for the miracle. He had provided because He really cared about *me*. I stood still for another few minutes and let this reality seep inside of me. Friendship with the Son of God was such a blessed experience.

Thinking back on the name and location of the hotel the Swedish man had told me about, I turned away from the docks and retraced my steps to where I had spoken with him five days earlier. It was easy to locate the hotel from there. When I entered the hotel, there were a number of people lingering in the lobby. One group was enthusiastically chatting away in Swedish! The familiar sound of this language eliminated some of the discomfort of hearing the English language being spoken all around me. Taking a chance, I approached the registration desk and asked in Swedish for a room for one night. To my delight, I was answered in Swedish. After paying for the room, I thanked the gentleman for his help and then wearily climbed the stairs to the room for a much-needed drink of water, a warm bath, a shave, and a good washing of my clothes. While my clothes were drying, I laid down on the soft bed and fell fast asleep, conceding to the fact that a meal would just have to wait until later.

Early the next morning I ventured downstairs and into the hotel's restaurant. I was very ready for some food. I sat down and ordered a breakfast of eggs and toast—the waiter was able to communicate with me in Swedish. I asked him if he knew of a Swedish or Finnish community in San Francisco. He mentioned that there was a Finnish Seamen's Mission located near the docks. He also knew of a Swedish Club that had started about two years ago. He wasn't sure where they were located, but he had heard previous customers talk about them. I thanked him for his information, finished my breakfast, and paid for it. I still had enough change for at least two more meals.

Finally, with food in my stomach and feeling rested after a good night's sleep, I headed back to the docks with renewed confidence. Intent on finding the Finnish Seamen's Mission, I wandered around, watching and listening. Heading east, I followed the coastline—full of port and ship activity. After about two miles of walking, I noticed some docks where ferryboats came and went across the water to the land masses east and north of San Francisco. I sat down on a bench and watched the ferryboats coming and going from the docks with their passengers. Most of the people appeared to be tourists, others looked to be local folks who probably worked in the adjacent land areas across the bay.

It was nearing noon, and my stomach was again beginning to feel hungry. While sitting on the bench lost in a blur because of the language barrier, I unexpectedly heard the familiar sounds of my own Finnish language. Immediately, I tuned in my ears to discover where the talking was coming from. Turning my head, I saw two men in work clothes walking from the ferry that had docked a few yards away from where I was sitting. I jumped up and made my way toward them, greeting them in Finnish as if I had known them for years. I received warm smiles and an eagerness from them to converse with me.

And this is how my friendship began with two men who had emigrated from Finland the previous year and who were in the process of becoming naturalized citizens of America. They worked at the docks loading and unloading cargo that was ferried across the water to the communities surrounding

San Francisco. I shared with them bits of my current situation and asked if they could help me find the Finnish Seamen's Mission. Laughing heartily and giving me a friendly slap on the back, they told me the mission was where they were boarding and, for now, called home. With enthusiasm they invited me to come and share some lunch with them at the eating hall of the mission. The doors for my future had just been opened to me. As I bowed my head to bless the food at lunch, I silently thanked my Friend for His reliable and merciful help in my behalf.

And so, my circumstances started to turn around. The Finnish Seamen's Mission was a haven for me, and with their instructions and help, I learned what I needed to do to become an American citizen. I learned that America would accept my declaration of intent to become a citizen. I had arrived on a ship. My name was on its crew list when the *Polwell* had arrived at the port of San Francisco on September 12. This information could be verified. Because of the war in Europe, my situation was favorably looked upon. I prudently followed the procedures at the properly designated times and filed the necessary paperwork with the Court of San Francisco for my initial application for United States citizenship. I found a class where I could learn to speak English, and I worked diligently to master this language, for citizenship in America depended on it. I was excited to be able to write and tell my family where I was and give them my address. I would finally be able to keep in touch with them and was anxious to eventually receive a letter from them.

The Finnish Seamen's Mission was also instrumental in helping me to find employment working at the ferry docks.

In November, the Panama-Pacific International Exposition ended. I had already been at the mission for two months and an opportunity arrived for a new job in Berkeley across the San Francisco Bay. There I worked at the Associated Oil Company attending to the boilers and pumping oil to the ships from the bulk plant. I chose to move to Berkeley so that I wouldn't have to ride the ferry back and forth to work each day. I was taken in as a boarder with a lovely Finnish family. The Finnish immigrants whom I was able to become acquainted with were very kind to me, and I did whatever I could do to help them. We all had a common goal of becoming honorable citizens in America, and we needed each other's help and camaraderie to make each other successful in this endeavor. These were wonderful human ties that enriched my life. Together we laughed, hoped, shared ideas and information, and basically looked out for each other.

In July 1916 I received my first letter from Elli. She and her husband had finally emigrated to America and were living in Buffalo, New York. It was wonderful to hear from her and to know that she was safe. Later that autumn, I received another letter from Elli telling me of the death of our brother, Pauli. He had received a gunshot wound to the head on a battlefield in France, later dying in a hospital in London. He was buried in the Nunhead (All Saints) Cemetery in London. My heart mourned for the brother I had never been able to meet. When I learned that he had fought with the Canadian Expeditionary Forces sent to France, I often wondered if he had been aboard the passenger ship from Canada that barely missed colliding with the naval merchant ship I was on in the English Channel. If so, that was the closest to him I was ever going to be, but I would never really know.

The grief my mother had to be enduring tore at my heart. Again, I sat down and wrote her another letter about losing a loved one. What could I say that would begin to lighten her deep sadness when I was aching also?

The Great War finally reached America. Germany's cruel indifference to human life by its use of unrestricted submarine warfare in attempt to break the Allied sea powers continued unrelentingly. Eventually, America was forced to abandon the neutral position it held regarding the war with Germany. In January 1917 Germany sent a telegram to their German ambassador in Mexico with a plan to involve Mexico in the war and to solicit Mexico's help in attacking America if America entered the war. The British intercepted this telegram and promptly apprised President Woodrow Wilson. Then, in mid-March, Germany deliberately torpedoed two American ships—the same day that the Provisional Government headed by Aleksandr Kerensky came into power in Russia following the Russian Revolution of late February in which the Russian people and the soldiers rebelled against the czar and his ineffectual leadership of the army.

On April 6, 1917, America, for its own reasons, declared war on Germany and became an "associated power" in the war. Immediately, America sent a small volunteer army, untrained for battle warfare, to France to assist the Allied Powers. Over the course of that year, only four American divisions were sent to France, none of which participated in any serious fighting. However, plans in America immediately went underway to mobilize and train men who could be transported to Europe to help the Allies on the battlefields in France. In May 1917,

Congress began to draft men into the armed forces. Within a few months more than ten million men had registered for military duty. It would be another year before America was ready to significantly play a role in being able to help the Allied Powers in the war.

On June 5, 1917, I went to the San Francisco precinct and registered for the draft, and then I waited. The draft was under a type of lottery system where names were randomly chosen from the registration pools for active duty. I wanted to do my part in the war, not only for America but also for Pauli, who had given his life for the Great War. During this year, I moved back closer to the San Francisco ferry docks where I lived as a boarder with another Finnish family and continued my job in Berkeley, taking the ferry to and from work each day.

And so, I waited for the day my name would come up and I would be officially drafted. English was getting easier for me to speak and read. Every day I purchased a newspaper so that I could read any articles written about the war, for I wanted to keep current about America's involvement. Every now and then I would receive a letter from Elli telling me about what was happening in Finland with our mother, but these letters arrived less and less due to the war conditions.

Since getting settled in America, I had written to my sweetheart in Finland, and I received a few letters in return. When I registered for the draft, I decided to write to her and end our relationship, for I wanted her to be able to find someone in Finland. My intentions were to become a citizen of the United States, and now I was committed to fight for America when my name was chosen to join the military. I felt it would be better for us both to break our exclusive ties. It was a difficult letter to write because she was a very special person to me. She responded back by letter that she understood and thanked me for the memories and times we had shared together. I never saw her or heard from her again.

A second revolution erupted in Russia in November 1917, causing civil war to soon break out in Finland. Because the Kerensky government was intent on supporting the Allied Powers and keeping Russia in the war—against the will of the Russian people and frustrated soldiers—this government was skillfully overthrown by the Bolshevik Party, and Vladimir Lenin became Russia's new leader. Lenin chose to listen to the people, and in December he began to negotiate an armistice with the Germans. Very early in March 1918, Russia was no longer one of the Allied Powers in the war; however, the armistice agreement with Germany included very harsh conditions. The choice for peace came with a heavy price with vast territorial areas ceded to Germany from Russian control, including Finland. With Russia no longer a threat to Germany, Germany now redirected troops with plans for a massive assault against the Allied Power troops of Britain, France, and the United States.

When the Bolshevik Party took power in Russia in November 1917, they also began to make promises to the middle-class workers of Finland regarding the productiveness of socialism. These promises gave nerve to many Finnish workers to begin a strike. It only took forty-eight hours for them to control most of Finland, causing intense negotiations with the Social Democratic Party of Finland to begin. Finally, after six intense days, the strike ended. In December Finland was successful in declaring its independence from Russia with a new middle-class government established. The new government was uncompromising toward the socialist aims of the Bolshevik Party and was determined to rule without them; however, civil war erupted in Finland at the very end of January 1918. The new Finnish government had appointed a military commander to establish law and order in Finland. This enraged the socialist-minded workers who were still sympathetic to the Bolshevik Party, causing them to again strike.

Because Russia had ceded Finland to Germany with its armistice agreements, Finland's new independent government received military help from Germany in the form of riflemen, equipment, and troop reinforcements to fight the socialist sympathizers. This caused a reign of terror to follow from these two fighting forces. During this civil war, ferocious independent murders and mass executions of many Finns took place until Finland's government finally took control of Helsinki in May 1918. Thousands of the Finnish socialist sympathizers ended up escaping to the Soviet Union. More than thirty thousand Finns died in less than four months in their own country. Three quarters of these died in executions and detention camps, while only one quarter died on the battlefield for territory within Finland during this civil war.

No family in Finland had escaped the suffering or death that this civil war had caused. In my own family, one of my relatives joined the socialist sympathizers and became a traitor to our family members. He was young and in the working-class of the Turku urban area, and he rallied with the efficacy of the socialist ideas of communism. I never found out if he was killed or if he was among those who escaped to Russia.

This was a fearful time for my mother and other members of my immediate family in Finland. Every day murders were taking place because traitorous motives were being carried out.

By the summer of 1918, ten thousand American troops a day started arriving in Europe, and, along with the Allied Powers, they began a series of strong counteroffensive attacks against which the Germans could not compete. American forces were actively participating on the battle lines. I finally received my draft orders and was inducted at the Presidio in San Francisco on July 24, 1918. My future as a soldier now hung in the balance.

War had inflicted stormy and hateful events into the lives of so many on earth. The accumulating atrocities and fears that continued to roll over individuals, countries, and continents were immeasurable in their impact upon lives. O yes, there was *much* bravery, tenacity, and determination of wills to fight for ideals that did not accommodate the selfishness of despotism. But coping with the unwanted changes and terrifying uncertainties forced upon societies by fighting for these ideals brought challenges to individuals—challenges one never thought they would be experiencing. The circumstances imposed by war had forever altered my own life in so many ways.

The one thing that mystified me the most was the safety that continued to surround me. Who was I—among the millions—to be constantly protected and guided through the dangers, perplexities, and fears that the storms of war had penetrated all of our lives? My only answer for this mercy was that my Friend and His Father loved me for reasons beyond my imagination. And knowing that much about Their love deepened my friendship with them. All I could do was, in love, gratefully bless Their holy names.

Later in my life I was introduced to two hymns which I was deeply drawn to. Their words melted my heart, for I truly understood their message about storms, cares, and love.

I know my heavenly Father knows

The storms that would my way oppose;

But He can drive the clouds away,

And turn my darkness into day,

And turn my darkness into day.

I know my heavenly Father knows

The balm I need to soothe my woes;

And with His touch of love divine

He heals this wounded soul of mine,

He heals this wounded soul of mine.

I know my heavenly Father knows

How frail I am to meet my foes;

But He my cause will e'er defend,

Uphold and keep me to the end,

Uphold and keep me to the end.

I know my heavenly Father knows

The hour my journey here will close;

And may that hour, O faithful Guide,

Find me safe sheltered by Thy side,

Find me safe sheltered by Thy side.

He knows, He knows

The storms that would my way oppose;

He knows, He knows,

And tempers every wind that blows

And tempers every wind that blows.[8]

---

8   S. M. I. Henry, "I Know My Heavenly Father Knows," (1897).

There's a wideness in God's mercy,

Like the wideness of the sea;

There's a kindness in His justice,

Which is more than liberty.

There is welcome for the sinner,

And more graces for the good;

There is mercy with the Savior;

There is healing in His blood.

For the love of God is broader

Than the measure of man's mind,

And the heart of the Eternal

Is most wonderfully kind.

If our love were but more simple,

We should take Him at His word;

And our lives would be all sunshine

In the sweetness of our Lord.[9]

~~~~~~~~~~~~~~~~~~~~~~~~~~~~~~~~~~~~

My Story

I have taken the time to contemplate Grandpa's experiences of weapon-filled seas and craggy hillsides sheltered with trees and a cave for hiding. I have wondered at the insecurities and adversities that accompanied his adoption of a new homeland. Great love carried him safely through every difficulty, and in return, he reverently acknowledged the Source of that great love for him. The gifts of faith and hope always remained his anchors—the gift of love the unwavering companion of his destiny. I have learned the validity of this exceptional truth— that love never ends and that it is the *greatest* of these three gifts that will never end.

---

9   Frederick W. Faber, "There's a Wideness in God's Mercy," (1854).

"Remember, O Lord, your great mercy and love, for they are from of old." Psalm 25:6

Providence

Grandpa's Story

On July 24, 1918, I received a letter in the mail from the United States Army instructing me to report to the Presidio in San Francisco. After saying good-bye to my very kind landlord and terminating my employment at the oil company, I reported for duty. And so, my induction into the U.S. Army began, along with the new routines of basic training and military life.

One evening in early August during my off-duty hours, I was walking across a footbridge on the beautiful grounds of the Presidio. Crossing the same footbridge in the opposite direction was my commanding officer walking with his girlfriend, and he was definitely enthralled by her company. I found this to be a charming situation on such a lovely evening, and so I saluted him and commented with a smile,

"Sir, a lovely evening to be with such a lovely lady." I kept on walking toward my barracks, thinking no more of the incident and receiving no reply from my commanding officer.

First thing the next morning I was surprised to be called in to see my commanding officer. I arrived and entered his office, saluted him, and announced my presence. His tone of voice and demeanor indicated that he was upset. He was incensed with me for making a comment about his girlfriend the night before, and because of my boldness, he ordered me to report for KP duty for the next two weeks as punishment. I was a bit baffled by his harshness, for I had meant no harm or indecency by my comment to him the evening before. But I gave him my sincere apologies and reported to the mess hall immediately for duty.

To be honest, I was relieved to be able to be in an eating environment again and not out marching and learning to use a riffle. However, knowing I was being punished, I did my very best to follow the orders of the sergeant in charge of the mess hall. I didn't want to cause any more problems. When the two weeks time for my punishment was up, I was surprised to learn that the mess sergeant had requested from his superior officer that I be transferred to work in the kitchen. He had noticed my abilities and was grateful for my experience in feeding large numbers of individuals every day, for he had begun to ask me how I had learned to work so efficiently in a kitchen. His request was granted, and I continued on working in the kitchen helping to prepare meals. This set into motion another change of events in my military life.

In early September I was given new orders. I was to be immediately transferred to Camp Lewis in Washington state to be in charge of the patient kitchen at the Camp Lewis Base Hospital. The hospital was able to care for three thousand patients, and currently many soldiers were being brought home from France with war injuries or pneumonia acquired on the battlefield. And so, I was put on a train for the very long ride from San Francisco to the station at Camp Lewis in Washington where I arrived on September 10, 1918.

Camp Lewis was built on a seventy thousand-acre piece of land near Tacoma, Washington. The land had been purchased and given as a gift to the federal government by local Tacoma citizens for use as an army base when America had entered the Great War in April 1917. In July of that year construction began, and in ninety days more than two thousand buildings had been built by ten thousand men. The 91st "Wild West" Division was the first to begin training at Camp Lewis in September until they were transported to France in June 1918, about one month before I was inducted into the army in San Francisco. Their first fighting in France began on the battlegrounds of the major "September Offensives" at St. Mihiel and Meuse-Argonne, where they were successful in breaking the German lines of battle.

Meanwhile, other regimens of soldiers continued to arrive at Camp Lewis for training, and when I arrived at the base, large numbers of soldiers were living in tents set up to accommodate the amount of men being trained there. This was the summer when America was transporting ten thousand troops a day to France to fight, and many of these troops were being sent from Camp Lewis.

Also during this time, large numbers of injured and sick soldiers were returning from France after fighting in the battle of Amiens and the second battle of Somme—major victories gained by the Allies during August—and the hospital at Camp Lewis was busy caring for many of these soldiers. The price that so many men paid with their injuries or loss of life for the Allied victories can never be measured or treasured enough. Again and again, I wondered at the turn of events that kept *me* from being sent to the battlefields of France. Why was I being shielded within the walls of an army base hospital kitchen? My profound gratefulness was always mingled with a curiosity for a reason that would explain this protection.

Another tragic complication occurring during these months was the great Spanish Flu Pandemic that was assaulting and killing people in the millions all over the globe. Many soldiers were returning to the hospital at Camp Lewis with this devastating influenza virus that caused pneumonia to develop. About one-third of our hospital staff eventually became sick with this virulent influenza, making care of the sick and wounded more challenging for the staff who were not ill. Again, I was spared and never got sick, but across America, thousands were losing their lives from this virus and others, strong enough to fight it when they became ill, still suffered from the difficult symptoms of this vicious illness. Incidentally, President Woodrow Wilson was one of the strong ones who successfully recovered from the virus after he became infected while negotiating the treaty of Versailles to end the war.

One evening after my work in the kitchen was done, I noticed a small group of men in uniform sitting together under a big tree on the grounds of Camp Lewis across from the hospital kitchen. What drew my attention to them was that they were reading a book and seemed to be having a stimulating discussion about what they were reading. I casually walked over to the group and started up a friendly conversation with them, eventually mentioning that I was curious about what they were reading. When they told me they were reading and discussing certain teachings from the Bible, I became even more curious.

That particular evening they were discussing the Bible's teaching on the seventh-day Sabbath. Of course, I began to counter their interpretation, saying that I was certain Sunday was the Sabbath and that I could show them from the Bible that this was so. They challenged me to find that information for them and to join them in two days for another discussion and share what I had discovered. I was excited about being able to help them, and I looked forward to our next meeting together. These were very pleasant men to have become acquainted with.

What I was unprepared for was the discovery that as I looked through my Bible I couldn't find anything that confirmed Sunday was the Sabbath. I was quite dumfounded with this predicament and couldn't wait to question the men further about this, because Christians everywhere I had been in my world travels regarded Sunday as the Sabbath and their day for worship. I was positive it had to be in the Bible somewhere.

When we met together two days later, I confessed that I hadn't been able to find anything yet that supported my firm belief in Sunday but that I was still searching. That evening the men showed me what the Bible reveals about the Sabbath, and I was unable to deny that this was the truth—especially when I learned that my Friend, Jesus, had worshipped on the seventh day when He was on this earth and that even His death and burial had honored the seventh-day Sabbath. I was exceptionally affected by my Friend's promise that I would be able to spend eternity with Him when He returns to this earth a second time to take those who choose to love and honor Him to heaven—to *His* home. In my Friend's heavenly home, I would be able to spend an eternity of Sabbaths with Him—all in His honor.

I asked more questions about what this unique group of soldiers knew about the Bible, and over the next few weeks, I was introduced to the most wonderful truths the Bible contained. I chose to fully embrace and believe in these truths, and in 1919 I was baptized into the Seventh-day Adventist Church in Tacoma, Washington, where I had begun to attend church with my new friends from Camp Lewis.

For the first time in my life, I felt energized about the future and the wonderful glories ahead. My future had a new purpose, and I wanted to live my life around that purpose. My Friend was teaching me to recognize and realize my life's mission. I finally understood how I could succeed in this mission, and the commitment I now embraced was unmovable. There was no turning away from a life mission of this magnitude—one that culminated in eternity with my Friend. There were others who needed to know about a friendship with Jesus of Galilee.

The Great War officially ended at 11 o'clock in the morning on November 11, 1918, and Camp Lewis was electric with excitement. For more than four long years the world had been occupied with the atrocities and impositions of war and fighting. The Allied Powers had finally defeated the Central

Powers, thus triumphing over the narcissism of despots and dictators. The relief was profound for those of us who had lived through the difficult challenges of the Great War and had fought for victory.

I stayed on at Camp Lewis until May 1919 when I was honorably discharged from the United States Army at the offices of the Presidio in San Francisco. It had been a privilege for me to serve America, for America was now the country I called home and would soon become a citizen of. As I sat on the train that took me back to San Francisco, I reflected on my Friend's perfect timing of events which had resulted in numerous blessings in my life. The reasons I had received so many interventions and provisions that had kept me alive and cared for came flooding over me.

I no longer needed to wonder why past events had happened as they did—for my faith, hope, and love had always been linked to Providence—the guiding force that mercifully influences the human with the divine. Providence had led me to the exact time and place where I would be given the opportunity to understand and accept the Bible truths that gave meaning and purpose to life—life that could continue throughout eternity with my Friend who cared so much about me. I knew there were many who would love to be introduced to my Friend, and I dedicated the rest of my life in service toward that endeavor.

The mysterious ways of Providence—the overarching wonders of God's care and guidance—reveal themselves in accordance with the timeline of heaven. Humans sometimes feel insignificant and without importance when the snarly cares and storms of life seem to suffocate or stonewall their desired outcomes. But when the real esteem of heaven for a human life is revealed and the distinction of worth is illuminated upon human hearts, then one will bow with devotion to this loyal Friend from heaven, knowing that God and His Son have always cared and will always care about them.

From the destitute toddler who was auctioned to a new home—one that taught me about a loving God—through my teens years when experiences and disappointments brought me to a cooking school, to my adult years spent on ships and perilous travels upon the sea, and further on to the reality of having to choose a new country to give my allegiance to and be willing to fight for, all led to the army base at Camp Lewis under a tree across from the hospital kitchen where I was introduced to friends who were willing to share with me truths from the Bible that changed my life forever. How could that have ever happened? There can only be one answer—Providence. And so today, the words of another song echo with magnificence what I now know to be veritable truth for my life.

God moves in a mysterious way

His wonders to perform;

He plants His footsteps in the sea,

And rides upon the storm.

Ye fearful saints, fresh courage take;

The clouds ye so much dread

Are big with mercy and shall break

In blessings on your head.

Judge not the Lord by feeble sense,

But trust Him for His grace;

Behind a frowning providence

He hides a smiling face.

His purposes will ripen fast,

Unfolding every hour;

The bud may have a bitter taste,

But sweet will be the flower.

Blind unbelief is sure to err,

And scan His work in vain;

God is His own interpreter,

And He will make it plain.[10]

~~~~~~~~~~~~~~~~~~~~~~~~~~~~~~~~~~~~~~

As I contemplate my life, the best thing I have learned is the reward my Friend promised many years ago as He left Galilee and returned to His homeland in heaven. He promised a home in heaven for those who have *faith* in His promise—*hope* in His return—and *love* for Him, the One who will make it all possible. One day He will return in the clouds accompanied by all of the angels in heaven and His Father. The sky will be gloriously lit with luminous lights a million times more beautiful than the Northern Lights flashing across the night skies in Finland.

Amid any and all storms in life, never lose faith, hope,

---

10   William Cowper, "God Moves in a Mysterious Way," (1774).

and love for the Friend who will make eternity possible for human beings who truly cling to their friendship with Him and by their actions prove their attachment to Him. That's why I am drawn to songs about storms, for they remind me to be strong and humble and willing to focus on the only Friend who can bring me through them and eventually take me to His home in heaven. I leave you now to contemplate and embrace the words of this last song, so full of hope, as we maintain our faith in a loving God kindly leading us home.

Let us sing a song that will cheer us by the way,

In a little while we're going home;

For the night will end in the everlasting day,

In a little while we're going home.

We will do the work that our hands may find to do,

In a little while we're going home;

And the grace of God will our daily strength renew,

In a little while we're going home.

The Songs

There's a rest beyond, there's relief from every
care,

In a little while we're going home;

And no tears shall fall in that city bright and fair,

In a little while we're going home.

In a little while, in a little while,

We shall cross the billow's foam;

We shall meet at last,

When the stormy winds are past,

In a little while we're going home.[11]

~~~~~~

My Story

I can still feel Grandpa's arms gently holding me on his lap. His stories about water, storms, craggy rocks, homelands,

11   Eliza E. Hewitt, "In a Little While We're Going Home," (1851-
      1920).

and cares have introduced me to his lifetime Friend—the Friend now waiting to make him a citizen of heaven according to the timeline of providence. One day soon that blessed day will become a reality and the resurrection of the dead in Christ will occur with spectacular effects.

I picture my grandpa in that new homeland with his Friend. Together they will visit the sea of glass and the river of life—places where eternal waters will continue to foster their friendship. Grandpa will sing a new song—the song of the Lamb, and their friendship will continue to grow throughout eternity. Today, after losing my grandfather nearly fifty years ago, I can say, "Yes, Grandpa, I want to be there with you, too. Thank you for telling me about your Friend."

Inside the cover of Grandpa's Bible was written this quotation: "Every jewel will be brought out and gathered, for the hand of the Lord is set to recover the remnant of His people, and He will accomplish the work gloriously."[12]

---

12   Ellen G. White, Early Writings (Washington, D.C.: Ellen G. White Publications, 1945), p. 70.

Postscript

I invite you to share these stories and sing these songs. I trust you have discovered the strength that faith promotes, the buoyancy that hope gives, and the warmth that love manifests. These three—faith, hope, and love—will last forever and are gifts from God whose providence provides an opportunity for guidance now and throughout eternity.

"Those who are wise will shine like the brightness of the heavens, and those who lead many to righteousness, like the stars for ever and ever." Daniel 12:3

Biographical Sketch

My grandfather was born in Rymättylä, Finland, on November 4, 1891, as Kustaa Adolf Engelbert Ackerman. His parents were William and Amalia Ackerman. Amalia was born on March 24, 1856; however, William Ackerman's date of birth is unknown. His father, William, died in 1893 when Kustaa was two years old. Kustaa's older sister, Elli, was born in 1887, and his younger twin brother and sister, Pauli and Anna, were born on June 10, 1894. Elli preceded Kustaa in death in 1945, Anna sometime after age nineteen (date unknown), and Pauli on August 25, 1916, during World War I.

When Kustaa was confirmed into the Evangelical Lutheran Church of Finland at the age of twelve, he changed his last name to Lehto. At age twenty Kustaa enrolled in the *Keittäjä ja Stuuerttikoulusta* cooking school full time in Turku, Finland, from 1909 to 1910, where he completed 2,000 class hours and graduated with his diploma cum laude.

He also completed the Board of Trade School for cooks and stewards and passed the Board of Trade Examination after completing 288 hours of training in September and October of 1911 in Hull, England.

Between 1910 and 1915 Kustaa sailed on various ships around the world for Finland and England, serving as a cook and steward. He arrived in San Francisco, California, on September 12, 1915 after completing a voyage from Maryport, England. It was then that Kustaa decided to make America his permanent home. He immediately found work at the Associated Oil Company in Berkeley, California, and learned to speak and become fluent in the English language. He worked at the Associated Oil Company until he was inducted into the United States Army.

Kustaa served in the United States Army as a private in the Medical Department from July 14, 1918, to May 28, 1919, during World War I, and was stationed at the Camp Lewis Army Base Hospital located near Tacoma, Washington, where he was in charge of the hospital kitchen as the mess sergeant.

During his military assignment, he became acquainted with Guy Jorgensen, one of the soldiers at Camp Lewis, who introduced Kustaa to the teachings of the Seventh-day Adventist Church. Kustaa was baptized in 1919 in Tacoma, Washington. From 1925 to 1956 Guy Jorgenson served as chemistry professor and department head of the Division of Science and Mathematics at Union College in Lincoln, Nebraska, where Jorgenson Hall was later named in his honor. Kustaa and Guy corresponded with each other for many years.

After his honorable discharge from the United States Army on May 28, 1919, Kustaa returned to the state of Washington.

He spent the summer of 1919 cooking at a camp for loggers in the Cathlamet area and also helped to build a friend's home. During this summer he continued taking classes to improve his English at the Cathlamet Washington High School. When September 1919 arrived, he started his freshman year at West Washington Missionary Academy (now Auburn Academy) located in the dense foothills of Mount Rainier thirty-five miles southeast of Seattle, Washington. This was the first year that West Washington Missionary Academy was open for students to attend.

In 1921 Kustaa transferred his academy studies to Broadview Academy in La Grange, Illinois, where he continued his schooling until his graduation on May 25, 1924.

After that, he worked at Broadview College as manager of the culinary department, bakery, and store. He managed these departments while also attending school full time. He continued working at this job while pursuing his college education at Broadview College in La Grange, Illinois. On May 25, 1929, he graduated with his bachelor of arts degree in languages and a minor in education. Kustaa was fluent in Finnish, Swedish, Norwegian, Danish, and English. He could read both Greek and Hebrew.

In June 1924 Kustaa attended and completed a Home Nursing Course that was sponsored by the Medical Department of the General Conference of Seventh-day Adventists, where he learned home hygiene, home nursing, and simple treatments.

Kustaa married Rhoda Christine Anderson on July 1, 1925. She was born in Enfield, Minnesota, on December 22, 1899. She grew up in a Seventh-day Adventist family and was baptized in October 1911 in Lock Lake in Enfield. When Rhoda met Kustaa, she was the librarian at Broadview College and had previously graduated from Broadview Theological Seminary in La Grange, Illinois, on May 31, 1921, with a bachelor of arts degree in education and library science. On April 14, 1927, Kustaa became a naturalized citizen of the United States.

In the summer of 1927, Kustaa and Rhoda sailed together on the passenger ship R.M.S. *Majestic* to Finland, Sweden, and England to visit family members and also to visit the grave of Kustaa's brother, Pauli, in a cemetery in London. Kustaa had taken the time to personally translate the book *Steps to Christ*, by Ellen G. White, into the Finnish language. He gave this copy to his birth mother, and before she died on September 12, 1931, in her homeland of Finland, she had accepted the beliefs of the Seventh-day Adventist faith.

In August 1930 Kustaa and Rhoda left La Grange, Illinois, and moved to Backus, Minnesota, to be closer to Rhoda's parents. They purchased a forty-acre farm and began the arduous task of rebuilding the old home on the property, finding gainful employment, and beginning their family during the years of the Great Depression.

Kustaa and Rhoda had five children—Vernon, Orville, Muriel, Charlotte, and Laila—whom they raised on their farm in Backus. Unfortunately, their son Orville was tragically killed in a car accident on May 21, 1954, at the age of twenty-two. At the writing of this book, there are twelve grandchildren, twenty-four great-grandchildren, and seven great-great-grandchildren alive.

In 1931 Kustaa built a service station on their property

at the Backus Corner where they were able to serve local customers and those passing by on U.S. Hwy 371. This service station was eventually closed in 1943; however, it did become the auto body shop for their son Vernon before he served in the Korean War.

Kustaa and Rhoda were instrumental in helping to establish and build the first Hackensack, Minnesota, Seventh-day Adventist Church eight miles north of Backus. The Hackensack church was officially organized on December 14, 1935. In 1938 the local church members raised three hundred dollars to purchase, with cash, the Devlin Garage building in Hackensack, Minnesota. The members had been renting the office of this garage and meeting together for the previous three years. When the garage became available for purchase in June 1938, the members rallied.

After purchasing the building on November 3, 1938, the remodeling of the building into a church officially began on September 28, 1939. Two years later, on September 27, 1941, the church was dedicated.

Today, the members of the Hackensack Seventh-day Adventist Church have a new church building that was constructed on the same piece of land after the Hackensack Fire Department did a controlled demolition burning of the original church. This church currently has a membership of seventy-two.

In December of 1938, Kustaa completed and received a certificate for attending the Layman's Bible Training Course in St. Paul, Minnesota, sponsored by the Home Missionary Department of the General Conference of Seventh-day Adventists. Kustaa had a desire to give Bible studies to individuals in the surrounding area, and he successfully used music filmstrips by evangelists Holley and Bond. These original filmstrip rolls remain in Kustaa's family and give heritage to the denominational materials available that he effectively used in lay evangelism during those years.

For the rest of his life, Kustaa remained very active in giving Bible studies and serving as an elder, deacon, and home missionary leader in the Hackensack church. Rhoda was the church clerk for many years and also served as a Sabbath School teacher, missionary volunteer leader, and organist. Records found in Rhoda's belongings after her death were of handwritten and typed Sabbath School programs she used or recorded. The average attendance at the Hackensack church during those years was between twenty-five and forty, with members and visitors included.

Church life was very important to Kustaa and his family. They always had a room in their home available for a minister who may be passing through and needed a place to stay. Many times the family would wake up and find a minister as their guest for breakfast, and they were gracious in caring for these individuals. At different time periods over a twenty-five year span, they cared for elderly members of their own family who could no longer live on their own.

Each year during the 1930s the Minnesota Conference of Seventh-day Adventists held camp meetings. Kustaa was always there for the full ten days with his family, for he was on staff as the main cook preparing the meals for those who attended the meetings.

From March 1936 until April 1942, Kustaa and Rhoda were both field workers for the Minnesota Historical Record

Society under the direction of the WPA (Works Project Administration). Together they researched and wrote the history of Cass County, Minnesota. From April until December of 1942, Kustaa worked for the WPA as a teacher of adult education, teaching classes in first aid and citizenship. This project was closed by the WPA during World War II.

In 1943 Kustaa became a cook at the Ah-Gwah-Ching State Sanitarium near Walker, Minnesota, which was located eighteen miles north of his home in Backus. This sanitarium was established as a tuberculosis hospital in 1907. It served as the Minnesota State Sanitarium until 1962. Kustaa worked there until April 1957 when he retired. Currently, Ah-Gwah-Ching is a state healthcare facility for geriatric patients. In 1946, Kustaa became the first aid chairman of Minnesota's Cass County Chapter of the American Red Cross, serving in this position for more than seven years. He held first aid Instructor certificates for teaching standard, junior, and advanced courses for the American Red Cross. He taught first aid classes for many years.

Over the years, Kustaa and Rhoda hired out the farmland on their forty acres until their son Vernon was old enough to farm it. In addition, they maintained and cared for milk cows and chickens. The milk, cream, eggs, and chickens—sold as fryers—helped to give their family extra income. Rhoda's many accomplishments included working as a seamstress, taking in more than twenty foster children throughout the years, and helping to establish the Backus Cemetery Association. Kustaa was listed in *Who's Who in Minnesota* and also in *Who's Who Among Americans of Finnish Descent*.

Kustaa passed away at 7:30 p.m. on May 29, 1962. He was

laid to rest in the Evergreen Cemetery in Backus, Minnesota, near his son Orville. His wife, Rhoda, passed away on January 11, 1988, and was buried beside him where they now await the second coming of Jesus.

Of interest is the historical fate of three of the four known ships that Kustaa sailed on around the world between the years of 1910 and 1915: The *Rhea* was torpedoed in September 1915 off Scilly Isles, an archipelago of islands twenty-eight miles off the southwest tip of England in the Celtic Sea. The *Fennia* was sunk by an Italian torpedo boat in 1941 during World War II. And the *Polwell* was sunk by a torpedo on June 5, 1918, off Rockabill Island in the Irish Sea. Records were not found regarding the fate of the *Njord*.

Photographs

Kustaa Lehto, 1911
Hull, England

Kustaa Lehto, 1959
Brainerd, Minnesota

Kustaa Lehto at Pauli's grave, 1927
London, England

Kustaa was able to visit his brother's grave in England eleven years after Pauli's death. Pauli enlisted in the 55th Battalion of the Canadian Expeditionary Force (CEF) on October 7, 1915 and on October 30, 1915, he sailed from Montreal, Canada aboard the *SS Corsican*, arriving in England on November 9, 1915. He was transferred to the 21st Battalion CEF on April 23, 1916 and was sent to France where he fought with the Allied Powers at Mount Sorrel. On June 13, 1916, he received a gunshot wound to the head, even though he was wearing a helmet. He later died, after a second surgery, at the King George Hospital in London at 4:00 a.m. on August 25, 1916.

Devlin Garage, 1938
Hackensack, Minnesota

First Hackensack Seventh-day Adventist Church
Dedicated in 1941
Hackensack, Minnesota

We invite you to view the complete
selection of titles we publish at:

www.TEACHServices.com

Scan with your mobile
device to go directly
to our website.

or write or email us your praises, reactions, or
thoughts about this or any other book we publish at:

TEACH Services, Inc.
P U B L I S H I N G
www.TEACHServices.com

P.O. Box 954
Ringgold, GA 30736

info@TEACHServices.com

TEACH Services, Inc., titles may be purchased in bulk for
educational, business, fund-raising, or sales promotional use.
For information, please e-mail

BulkSales@TEACHServices.com

Finally, if you are interested in seeing
your own book in print, please contact us at

publishing@teachservices.com

We would be happy to review your manuscript for free